CONTENTS

PREFACE

Are you looking for an edge?

Do you lift weights to make your muscles stronger? Sprint to run faster? Perform plyometrics to jump higher? Are you making progress, but not as fast as you'd like? We often hear coaches and commentators use adjectives such as "explosive," "powerful," and "gifted" to describe their best athletes. But how did they get that way?—there has to be more to success than God-given talent. More importantly, how can *you* reach the outer limits of your genetic potential? The answer is complex training.

Complex training is a workout system that combines strength work and speed work for an optimal training effect. It gives you the maximum results in the shortest amount of time. You must work hard to achieve your goals, but there are two kinds of work: hard work and smart work. This book will show you how to work smart using the principles of complex training.

Explosive Power and Strength: Complex Training for Maximum Results is organized into three parts. The first deals with the origins of complex training and explores the physiological reasons behind this exciting new training method. The second part shows you how to perform various resistance training and plyometric training exercises safely and effectively. The proper coupling of resistance and plyometric work is at the heart of complex training. The final part ties it all together by giving you several examples of complex training workouts and showing you how to develop your own complex training regimen.

If you have sought out all the possible ways to improve your performance but have never tried complex training, this book, written in easy-to-understand language, will introduce you to an exciting new training method. Complex training is not the only way to become a better athlete, but it's the *best* way.

Explosive Power and Strength is your edge.

PART I

A BETTER WAY
TO TRAIN

Exercise scientists define power as "the optimal combination of speed and strength to produce movement." Power is what enables the superstar running back to break tackles, the Olympic sprinter to explode out of the blocks, and the dominating tennis player to serve ace after ace. Power is what separates the medal winners from the also-rans, and it's power that will make you a winner too.

Some athletes lift weights to develop power, some perform plyometrics, and some do both. The typical conditioning program consists of lifting weights three times a week and performing plyometrics on the off days. Many athletes perform plyometrics at the beginning of their workouts as a warm-up. Others perform plyometrics on the same day, doing plyos in the morning and lifting in the evening. All these methods will increase power, but not very effectively.

Complex training develops power in a very sport-specific manner. *Functional training* is the new buzz word in athletic conditioning. It's simply a much better approach to preparing your body for the demands of a specific sport. Unlike conventional programs that have little carryover to athletics, especially those that rely primarily on machine exercises, the power developed with complex training is immediately applicable to sport. In fact, the power increases achieved through complex training are up to three times more effective than conventional training programs!

Complex training consists of four components: resistance training, plyometric training, sprint training, and sport-specific training. Chapter 1 will examine each of these components. Worked separately, these components will make a good athlete; worked together through complex training, they will make a great athlete. Chapter 2 will show you the physiological reasons why complex training is a better way to train.

CHAPTER
1

COMPLEX TRAINING COMPONENTS

Many athletes are married to tradition in the weight room, believing that the only training that should be performed there is weight training. Although they may concede that a small area for stretching is permissible, the weight room is sacred ground meant for squats, bench presses, and curls. Weight rooms are for weights; that's why they're called weight rooms. Despite their narrow-minded philosophy, these athletes enjoy good results from their training.

Athletes who are more open-minded use a combination of resistance training and plyometrics over the course of their weekly schedule. Some even break tradition and perform plyometrics in the weight room! These athletes enjoy better results from their training. Finally, there are athletes who combine weight training and plyometrics into the same workout session, using plyos not as a warm-up performed early in the workout, which is usually the case, but performing them between sets or even as part of a weight training set. If a workout calls for four sets of squats, they'll perform depth squats or repeat standing long jumps between sets. These athletes perform complex training, and they enjoy the best results from their training.

Complex training was developed by the Europeans to blend the results of heavy weight training with what they call "shock training" and what we call plyometrics. Plyometrics follows the theory that the body has an arousal mechanism that enables an athlete to take advantage of the body's capacity for physical output. Consequently, many European exercise textbooks showed athletes performing various hopping, skipping, jumping, and throwing exercises designed to stimulate this arousal mechanism. It worked, and for many years plyometrics was the training method deemed most effective for taking athletes to a higher level of performance.

"For many years the Russians and Eastern Europeans have supplemented the training of their competitive athletes with systematic supplementary training in other sports," says South African exercise scientist Mel Siff in his textbook, *Supertraining*. "For instance, Olympic weightlifters and field athletes have included volleyball or basketball in their overall training regimens." Unfortunately, for most U.S. athletes, this type of training "generally has not advanced scientifically much beyond the way in which it was used several decades ago, and the choice of combinations, duration, intensities and periodization is often guesswork," according to Siff.

To ensure that supplementary training is a plus for your athletic development rather than a minus, you must first understand the components of this training method. I call these the building blocks of complex training. Knowing the advantages and disadvantages of each building block will enable you to "plug in" the right combination of exercises in your training to fulfill your needs. For example, if you're a strength and power athlete such as a football player or a shot-putter, it wouldn't make sense to perform five minutes of stationary cycling between heavy sets of squats. And if you are a distance runner, it wouldn't make sense for you to spend two hours a day in the weight room trying to look like Arnold.

Although there are many types of training, for simplicity, I've narrowed down the building blocks into four general categories. As you progress in the complex training system, you can add more subcategories to your training arsenal. For now, however, the categories I want you to be concerned about are plyometrics, resistance training, sprint training, and sport-specific training.

◆ Resistance Training

When we talk about resistance training, most of us think about weight training. Although it's true that weight training is one form of resistance training, anything that makes a muscle work harder can be classified as resistance training. Stretching using surgical tubing is resistance training. Throwing medicine balls is resistance training. So is performing calisthenics, which uses your own body weight for resistance.

With all the various sophisticated hydraulic and isokinetic resistance training machines available, some weight rooms don't even have free weights. That's unfortunate, because the advantage of free weights is that you can precisely determine the resistance and target specific muscles. With machines you can do this also, but when you change machines, you have to contend with different cables and cams, making it difficult to judge progress. Also, because machines do not involve the stability required of free weight training, there is less strength transfer to athletics.

Strength training accomplishes the first half of the complex training equation, with plyometrics, sprint training, and sport-specific training completing it. By itself, strength training will produce results, but not to the same level. Several years ago, I had an Olympic javelin thrower and two strong football players working out together. The football players could bench press about 400 pounds; the javelin thrower never did the exercise but did various forms of complex training. As a test, I had them perform a seated medicine ball chest pass for distance. I specifically chose this exercise because it resembled a bench press motion. The football players threw 28 and 32 feet, respectively. The javelin thrower threw it 48 feet before it hit the wall! Although the football players had strength, and no doubt the strength base to throw far, they could not effectively use their strength because they did not train explosively.

Strength training raises the body's ability to excite the motoneurons by nearly 50 percent. This gives the nervous system more involvement in the workout and prepares the muscles for even greater challenges. However, the activity has to be a high-intensity session of strength training to achieve the best results. As with plyometrics, quality is more important than quantity. The resistance training portion of the complex training model will therefore consist of low repetitions of moderate to heavy loads, as they produce the greatest amount of motoneuron firing and preparation for plyometrics. For example, if you're working your upper body pushing muscles, you could perform three reps with as heavy a load as possible in the bench press followed by a medicine ball chest pass exercise for the same muscles.

◆ Plyometrics

What is plyometrics? Plyometrics consists of hopping, skipping, jumping, and throwing activities designed to make you faster—that's a simple definition, but it will work for now. During the plyometric component of complex training, you must train at maximum speeds; submaximal efforts will only produce submaximal results. This is an application of the law of specificity: If you want to compete at higher speeds, you must train at higher speeds. If you train at slower velocities, you will teach your muscles to perform at these slower velocities. Remember the ankle weights popular many years ago? They violated the specificity principle because they changed the running style—a study at San Diego State proved this—and made you run at a slower velocity. In effect, ankle weights will train you to run more slowly. Likewise, running in sand—a popular training method that is being promoted by many U.S. coaches—also violates the law of specificity. Although sand training can be useful for strengthening the ankles and hamstrings, the leg turnover is so slow that if you overdo it, you will train your muscles to run more slowly.

Going from slow muscles to fast muscles requires performing quick, "explosive" movements. These activities must allow for minimal contact with the ground (lower body) or the hand contact surface (upper body). Plyometrics is the best answer for these types of exercise needs. Lower body plyometric exercises emphasize quick foot movements and the ability to get off the ground quickly. Upper body plyometric exercises emphasize using medicine balls to teach the muscles to respond more quickly to external forces.

◆ Sprint Training

From a theoretical standpoint, speed of movement in running depends on two factors: stride length and stride frequency. Stride frequency is generally considered to be largely dependent on the type of muscle fiber the athlete has. Faster fibers give an athlete an advantage in the quality and speed of muscle contraction. Slower fibers provide an advantage in maintaining work over prolonged periods.

If an athlete can't make significant improvements in stride frequency by pushing harder and faster off the ground, he or she looks toward improving stride length. This is usually the case because it is so difficult to improve stride frequency. (It has been estimated that although you can increase a muscle's strength by 300 percent, you can only increase its speed by approximately 10 percent!) Increasing stride length allows athletes to cover the same distance as athletes with greater stride frequency in the same amount of time, thereby offsetting their competitors' advantage.

How do you go about increasing the ability to push off the ground with more power? To get to this point, you have to take a course slightly different from the norm: The workouts may be shorter but of higher intensity. *Quality is the key, not quantity.* The athlete will also have much longer rest periods. Short workouts with long rest periods may sound like a great deal at first, but these workouts are extremely stressful on the nervous system.

◆ Sport-Specific Training

Attempts have been made to condition for sports by copying the movements that occur in sports. You'll find weighted footballs, uphill and downhill running courses, and skating machines. A better idea is to stimulate the fibers you want with resistance training, then perform sport-specific movements. For example, a basketball player could do a heavy set of leg presses followed by repeated rim jumps. This approach will ensure that technique is not compromised, which will happen with the other methods. In fact, it has been shown that if a runner trains on a surface with more than a two percent incline, technique will be altered significantly. Again, the law of specificity.

The essence of complex training is that athletes must do more than just build muscle to increase strength: They need to train the nervous system as well. Complex training allows athletes to work the muscles in conjunction with the nervous system in such a way that the slow muscle fibers behave like the faster fibers. The next chapter examines how complex training accomplishes this.

CHAPTER

2

COMPLEX TRAINING PHYSIOLOGY

To understand fully how to use complex training requires not only knowing its components, but also having a general knowledge of the body's energy and movement systems. It's not that you need to know the names and functions of every muscle group—although there is no harm in learning—but you should have an overall perspective on how your muscular, nervous, and cardiovascular systems work together.

◆ The Muscular System

The human body contains both fast-twitch and slow-twitch muscle fibers. Slow-twitch fibers are called type I and are capable of producing submaximal force over extended periods. These are the fibers athletes involved in aerobic activities (such as distance running) want to develop.

Fast-twitch fibers are classified as type IIa and type IIb and are capable of producing maximal force for brief periods. These are the types of fibers strength and power athletes such as football players and sprinters want to develop. The difference between these two fibers is that the type IIa have more endurance characteristics whereas the type IIb have more speed characteristics. In many sports, both fibers are used, with the type IIb contracting first. For example, a speed skater would begin a 1,000-meter race by recruiting the type IIb fibers; then, as these fibers fatigued, the type IIa fibers would take over. There is another type of fiber called type IIc that can develop the characteristics of either fast- or slow-twitch fibers with training.

Despite the implied preference a strength and power athlete would have for predominantly fast-twitch fibers, both are important to the athlete's overall development. Fast-twitch fibers give the athlete the ability to move quickly and explosively. Slow-twitch fibers are responsible for the stabilization and posture the athlete needs when performing any movement. In other words, they provide the stability to make the action complete.

In the context of complex training, the primary goal of a strength and power athlete is to first emphasize the type IIb fibers and get the type IIc fibers to act like type IIb fibers. The type IIa fibers, although called fast twitch, are often not especially useful for many athletes. Power lifters and bodybuilders, for example, have highly developed type IIa fibers but cannot display their strength quickly. Here's another example. Hamstring strength is of primary importance to sprinters, and this muscle group is composed mainly of type IIb fibers. As proof, if you look at the hamstring development of sprinters, you often find they have better development than bodybuilders.

The resistance training exercises chosen for this complex training program will increase athletes' strength and thus their stability. This is important to overall athletic development and will be especially significant for injury prevention. However, as athletes reach the higher levels of conditioning, they must reduce the quantity of type IIa work and concentrate on type IIb work.

The wonders and vast potential of the human body are often ignored, even in the minds of most elite athletes. When properly challenged, the human body has the capacity to make significant changes, one of which is a change in how muscle fibers function. Research shows that it is possible to train a fast-twitch muscle fiber to behave like a slow-twitch fiber, and vice versa. (Consequently, athletes involved in aerobic sports must be careful not to include too much training for fast-twitch fibers or they will risk teaching their slow-twitch fibers to behave like fast-twitch fibers.) However, both of these changes are difficult to bring about and require a great amount of work. Interestingly, the reasons for each being a challenge are completely different.

The difficulty in training the muscles comes about as a result of daily life. On any given day, the activities a human being performs during the course of a normal routine—walking across the room, washing dishes, lifting a stack of books—are completed at such slow speeds that they condition the body to function slowly. Thus, everything else an athlete does outside of training actually hinders the progress he or she makes in a program intended to develop faster muscles. For every two steps forward taken in the gym, count one step back for living the rest of life outside of it. Fortunately, the fast-twitch fibers an athlete already possesses are even more resistant to change. To turn a fast muscle into a slow one, the athlete needs a constant quasi-static resistance training program. Exercise bouts would consist of fewer repetitions of heavy loads at low speeds, leaving higher speed and explosive work completely out of the standard regimen.

The muscular system works like a computer system in that whatever an athlete puts into it is what the athlete gets out of it. Muscles want to complete a task in the most efficient way they know how. If an athlete only teaches the muscles to complete the task slowly, that's what the athlete will get back. It follows then that an athlete who needs to compete at higher speeds needs to train the muscles to function optimally at these higher speeds. Training at lower speeds will not be effective for developing power. That's why tennis players don't make a six-mile run a regular part of their workout; it serves little purpose in a sport with such a large anaerobic component.

◆ The Nervous System

If the muscular system is the computer, the nervous system is the software. The nervous system triggers a muscle's response to a stimulus, telling it what to do and when to do it. The neurons also tell a muscle fiber whether it should behave like a fast-twitch or a slow-twitch fiber.

Physically training an area of the body calls on that area's motor units. A motor unit consists of the three elements shown in figure 2.1: the motoneuron, which tells the muscles to contract; its motor axon, which takes the information from the central nervous system and gives it to the muscle fiber; and the muscles that are told to contract at the end of the communication line. Motoneurons tend to be attached to more than one muscle fiber, varying from the 5 to 10 range to more than 100 and up to 1,000, depending on the area of the body. When a single motoneuron is excited, all of the muscle fibers attached to it are stimulated simultaneously.

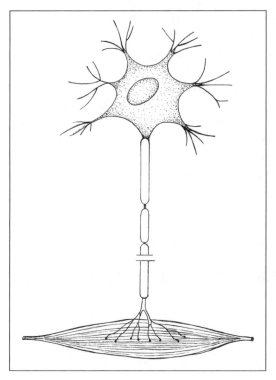

Fig. 2.1.   A motor unit. Adapted, by permission, from J. North, 1992, Motor units. In *Strength and power in sport*, edited by P.V. Komi (Champaign, IL: Human Kinetics. Copyright 1992 by International Olympic Committee).

The stimulation process is similar to lighting a fuse on a package of firecrackers. The central nervous system sparks the process, sending the signal down the axon toward the muscle fibers. At the end of the axon is the synapse, which holds the chemical acetylcholine (ACh) in little pouches. The pools of ACh then jump over to the muscle membrane, where the ACh generates the explosion of an electrical impulse throughout the muscle fiber. The better trained the athlete, the more efficient the process.

A comparison of two athletes shows that the specifically trained athlete has a distinct advantage in the firing of motoneurons. A trained hurdler and a runner trained only in flat running decide to race each other in the hurdles; both have the same leg speed in a flat race. The hurdler has learned the proper techniques of the hurdling motion, so his or her motoneurons are able to fire quickly at each moment that a reaction is needed. The motoneurons of the flat sprinter fire more haphazardly over the course of the race, making the athlete less effective in this competition, even though he or she may be as fast or faster over 100 meters.

To capitalize on a muscle's utmost potential to gain strength and speed, an athlete must raise the level of excitement in the muscle fibers and challenge them when they reach their highest levels. This is a two-step process in an athlete's conditioning program, and each step is equally important.

Once the motoneurons are fired up (through resistance training), it's time to teach the muscles to function at their highest possible speeds. The second half of the workout will thus be a plyometric exercise, matched to stimulate the muscles awakened during the resistance training exercise by performing a related or specific explosive movement similar to the resistance exercise.

◆ The Neuromuscular Connection

Complex training matches pairs of exercises from two sources: a resistance training pool and a plyometric pool. The resistance exercises will be of the traditional variety (e.g., squats, lunges, and various dead lifts). This group of exercises is so broad based as to complement a large selection of plyometric exercises. Depending on the sport, the season, and which muscles need to be worked on any given day, the athlete will be able to arrange a large number of combinations. Not only will the constantly changing apparatus keep the athlete interested in the training program, but the variety will make the workouts more effective. The more varied the workout, the less chance the body has to adapt to any one way of training. This will be key in building speed and thus power.

The number of muscle fibers an athlete has and the types of fiber in these muscles are both important factors. However, it is the neural factors that give the body the "jump start" that allows the training process to begin. As the conditioning process continues, the nervous system learns the necessary skills and hypertrophy takes over the limelight. Before getting to that point, the athlete—remembering that he or she doesn't need to bulk up—needs to find a way to arouse the nervous system quickly to get the most out of the workout. This is where tricking the body comes in.

That gifted athlete who everyone loves to hate has probably inherited a predominance of fast-twitch muscle fibers. Many athletes have predominantly slow-twitch muscle fibers, making it difficult to start, accelerate, and change direction quickly. Complex training allows the athlete to work the muscle fibers in conjunction with the nervous system in such a way that the slow-twitch fibers are taught to behave like fast-twitch fibers.

You may have noticed by now the repeated references to "teaching" the muscles. This concept is known as motor learning, and it is a segment of the training process dominated by the nervous system. By plugging into a high-intensity training system, the nervous system will be maximally excited and ready to accept the benefits that resistance training and plyometrics offer the athlete.

◆ The Cardiovascular System

So much emphasis has been placed on aerobic training in the United States that it has become a dominant component of most conditioning programs. However, except in the early stages of their careers, aerobic training for strength and power athletes is out of the question. Aerobic training *may* help an athlete recover from high-intensity exercise, but it does so at the expense of speed and power and increases the risk of overuse injuries and overtraining. Endurance training is important, but do only as much as absolutely necessary and be certain that the type of endurance developed is specific to the sport.

PART II

COMPLEX TRAINING EXERCISES

The chapters in this section present the resistance training and plyometric training exercises that you will perform in matched pairs to form the core of your personal complex training program. Each of the 80 exercises is described and illustrated for you. Please pay careful attention to the individual techniques provided as well as to the general precautions that precede each exercise index. Flaws in exercise technique may lead to serious injuries. The last thing an athlete wants is to be injured during workouts, so learn the proper execution of each lift and exercise you intend to perform before starting your program. Follow the performance guidelines in these chapters and you'll go a long way toward achieving your goals quickly and safely.

CHAPTER
3

RESISTANCE
EXERCISES

Many gyms consist primarily of resistance training machines because of their attractive designs and because they can often be used with minimal supervision. However, proper instruction is always important with any resistance training exercise to avoid injury and increase effectiveness.

◆ Machines

Virtually all gyms carry several pieces of exercise machines from a major equipment company. Common names include Nautilus, Eagle, CAM II, Hammer, Hydrafitness, Universal, Arcuate, and Polaris. Often no free weights are available in these facilities, only machines. If this is the case, you must do your best to substitute a free weight exercise with the appropriate machine exercise. For example, use the leg press to replace the squat and the Smith machine shoulder press to replace the barbell military press.

Most machines use weight for resistance in the form of fixed, adjustable weight stacks or a carriage that can be loaded with weight plates. Other forms of resistance come from hydraulic cylinders, water canisters, and air pressure. Although many machines can be adjusted to fit a variety of body types, tall and short people often will find that many machines will not fit their frames. The lowest bench press supports can be out of reach for some women. And if you're under five feet, it's not uncommon to run across leg curl and seated calf machines that don't account for your less-than-average lower leg length. Although manufacturers are responding to this need, expect to encounter some frustrations with a gym that features primarily machines.

The following performance guidelines apply to almost every exercise machine:

• Position yourself in a straight, aligned manner by adjusting the seat and the backrest. Generally, the center of the body part you're working should be aligned with the center axis of the pulley apparatus.

• Avoid any jerky or sudden movements when lifting, and do not twist or shift your weight during the exercise. Also, do not lean forward or arch your back when using equipment that makes you exercise while seated.

• If seat belts are available on a machine, use them.

• Read all warning signs and any additional instructions provided on a machine. Do not use any machine that is not functioning smoothly, and report the problem immediately to the appropriate personnel.

• If your gym has equipment you have never used, avoid experimentation. Insist that an instructor go one-on-one with you so you can derive maximum benefit from the exercise. Because every machine has its own peculiarities, ask the experts about these machines rather than trying to figure them out for yourself.

• And, if you have a chronic injury, you may need to avoid certain exercises that aggravate the condition.

◆ Free Weights

In addition to barbells and dumbbells, the category of free weight equipment includes accessory apparatus such as benches and squat racks. With few exceptions, an exercise performed with free weights is always superior to an exercise performed with a machine. The following guidelines apply to free weight exercises:

• Always use collars. The most durable collars for the longer Olympic and power lifting bars snap on with levers, such as the "E-Z on" type. (The best way to test a collar is to try it. You should be able to secure any weight plate to the end of a barbell and tilt it on end without the plate falling off.)

• Most gyms have fixed dumbbells in that the collars are welded to the bar. However, you should always inspect any dumbbell before using it to make certain the plates are secure.

• When performing any exercise that has you lying on your back, always use a spotter. It's also a good idea to have a spotter for any heavy leg exercise that has you resting the barbell on your shoulders, such as the back squat.

• If your feet do not touch the ground when lying on a bench press bench, or if the height is such that it causes you to arch your back excessively, place weight plates or other objects under your feet so they are firmly fixed to a surface.

• Squat racks should be adjusted to a height about four inches below shoulder level.

ABDOMINAL CURL WITH PULLEY

Procedure: 1. Kneel in front of a high pulley machine with your back facing the machine.

2. Using a rope harness, place each end of the rope over your shoulders and grasp the knotted ends.

3. Keeping your hips stationary, curl forward from the waist as far as comfortable, and then slowly return to the start.

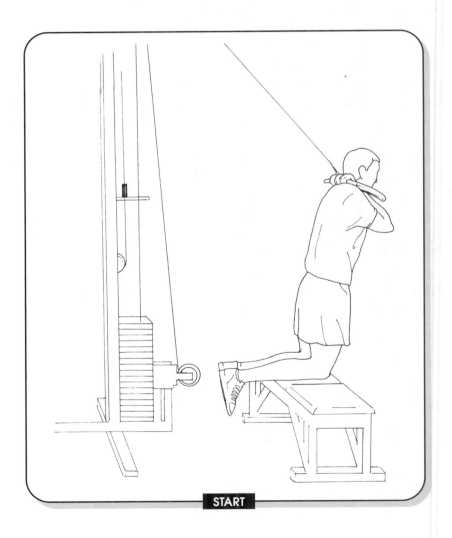

START

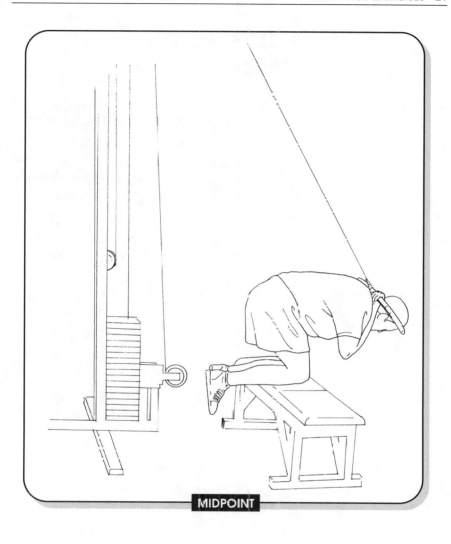

MIDPOINT

ALTERNATING DUMBBELL PRESS

Procedure: 1. Stand with your feet shoulder-width apart and hold a dumbbell in each hand, palms facing forward.

2. Press one dumbbell overhead and slightly in toward the midline of your body. As you lower the weight, press the other weight overhead in the same manner.

3. Continue alternating in this manner, performing an equal number of repetitions for each arm.

BACK SQUAT

Procedure: 1. With a barbell resting behind your neck, spread your feet shoulder-width apart and point your toes slightly out (start).

2. Take a deep breath and bend your legs in a slow, controlled manner until the tops of your thighs are at least parallel to the floor (midpoint). During the descent, keep your back flat and locked in extension, your chest out, and your eyes focused slightly downward or directly ahead.

3. Drive back up to the start, exhaling when your legs are nearly straight. During the ascent, look directly ahead or slightly up.

START/FINISH

(continued)

MIDPOINT

BENCH PRESS

Procedure: 1. Lie face up on a bench press bench with your feet flat on the floor, straddling the bench with your feet shoulder-width apart.

2. Remove the barbell from the supports so it is suspended directly above your throat. Your wrists should be positioned over your elbows (start).

3. Take a deep breath and lower the weight to mid-chest, or slightly lower if you're female (midpoint).

4. Without bouncing the weight off your chest, press it back to the start, exhaling when your arms are nearly straight. Note that the path of the bar forms a slight arc.

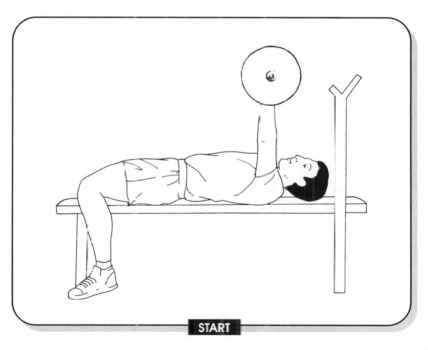

START

(continued)

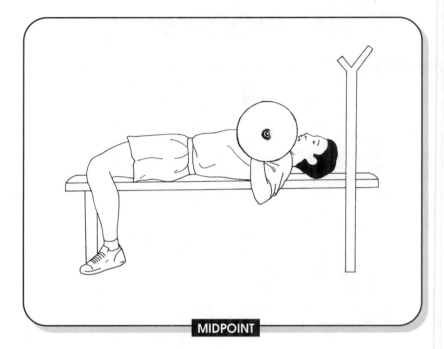

MIDPOINT

BENT-OVER ROW

Procedure: 1. Grasp the barbell with an overhand grip.

2. Keeping your chest out and head slightly up, bend over until your back reaches a 45-degree angle to the floor.

3. Begin the exercise by pulling the weight with your arms until it reaches the bottom of your rib cage, then slowly lower the weight by extending your arms.

START

(continued)

MIDPOINT

FRONT RAISE

Procedure:
1. Grasp a barbell with your palms facing you.

2. Keeping your arms straight but not hyperextended, raise the weight until your arms are parallel with the ground without leaning backward.

3. Lower the weight slowly without bending your arms to return to the start.

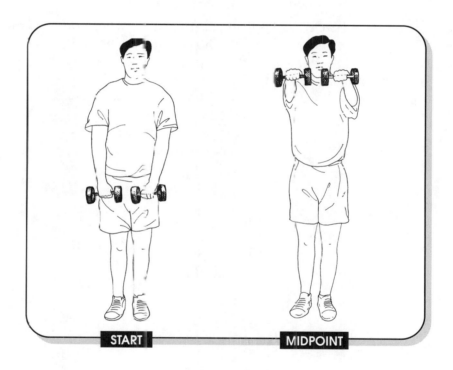

START   MIDPOINT

FRONT SQUAT

Procedure: 1. With a barbell resting on the front of your shoulders, spread your feet shoulder-width apart and point your toes slightly out (start).

2. Take a deep breath and bend your legs in a slow, controlled manner until the tops of your thighs are at least parallel to the floor (midpoint). During the descent, keep your back flat, your chest out, your elbows up, and your eyes focused slightly downward or directly ahead.

3. Drive back to the start, exhaling when your legs are nearly straight. During the ascent, look directly ahead or slightly up.

START

MIDPOINT

GLUTE-HAM RAISE

Procedure: 1. On a back extension bench, assume the starting position shown. Most of these benches have a pad above your ankles (prevents raising your legs) and a rear footpad (prevents slipping forward). If you do not have access to a back extension bench, lie lengthwise on a bench or sturdy table and have someone hold your legs while you perform the movement. Placing a rolled-up towel under your hips often makes this variation more comfortable.

2. Perform the exercise by bending as far forward from the waist as possible (without rounding your back) and then arching back upward.

3. When you reach a parallel position, continue the movement by lifting your torso to the position shown (finish).

4. Reverse this procedure and bend forward to return to the start.

Note: For added resistance, clutch a weight across your chest.

START

FINISH

GOOD MORNING

Procedure: 1. Place a lightweight barbell on the back of your shoulders and spread your feet hip-width apart.

2. Keeping your chest out and your head in line with your spine, slowly push your hips backward while keeping your spine slightly extended until you feel your body weight centered on your toes.

3. At this point, stop and return to the starting position by pushing your hips forward.

START   MIDPOINT

HIGH PULL

Procedure: 1. Start with the bar resting on your thighs, just above your knees, and use an overhand grip. Spread your feet hip-width apart or slightly wider, whichever is most comfortable. Look straight head and keep your back slightly arched.

2. Begin the exercise by straightening your legs (not your back) until the bar reaches the middle of your thighs.

3. Continue the movement by straightening your knees and back completely, then shrugging your shoulders, then pulling the bar to the lower part of your rib cage with your arms.

4. Return the bar to the start by allowing it to drop to midthigh and then slowly lowering it to the position just above the knees.

START

(continued)

MIDPOINT

FINISH

HIP CRUNCH

Procedure:
1. Sit on an exercise mat with your knees bent and your upper body supported on your hands.
2. From this position, rotate your hips up and back until your knees come in contact with your chest and your abdominals are completely flexed.
3. Slowly return to the starting position while lowering your legs but keeping your abdominals tight as long as possible.

For added resistance, hold a medicine ball between your knees.

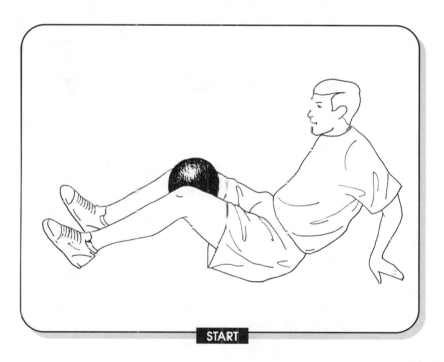

START

(continued)

MIDPOINT

HIP ROTATOR

Procedure: 1. Lie face up with your arms extended to the sides.

2. Keeping your feet together to form a 90-degree angle at your knees, lift your legs until your thighs are perpendicular to the floor.

3. Begin the exercise by rolling your legs to the right as far as comfortable and then to the left.

Try to touch your knees to each side. Do not lift either shoulder off the ground. For added resistance, hold a medicine ball between the knees.

(continued)

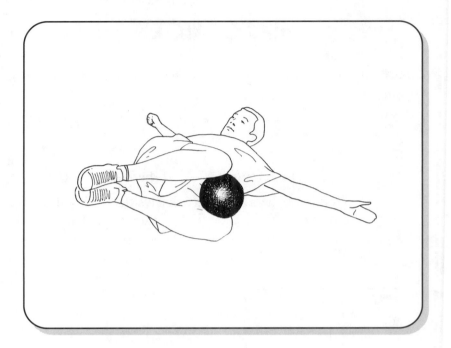

INCLINE BENCH PRESS

Procedure: 1. Lie face up on an incline bench with your feet flat on the floor. (If no seat is available, bend your knees slightly as shown.)

2. Remove the barbell from the supports so it is suspended directly above your forehead (start).

3. Lower the weight to a point just below your collarbone (midpoint) and then press it back to the starting position. Exhale when your arms are nearly straight.

START

(continued)

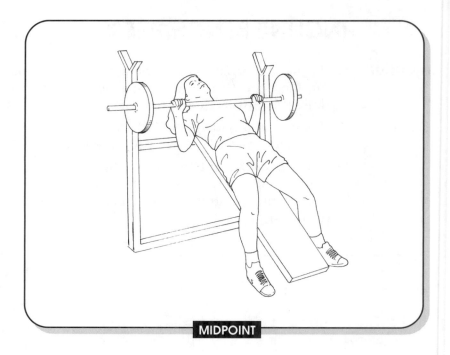

MIDPOINT

INCLINE ROW

Procedure:

1. Lie face down on a bench that is inclined 30 to 45 degrees. Let your arms hang perpendicular to the ground while grasping dumbbells in each hand.

2. Lift the weights so that your arms extend behind your back. Be sure to pinch your shoulder blades together tightly.

3. Return to the starting position by controlling the descent of the weights

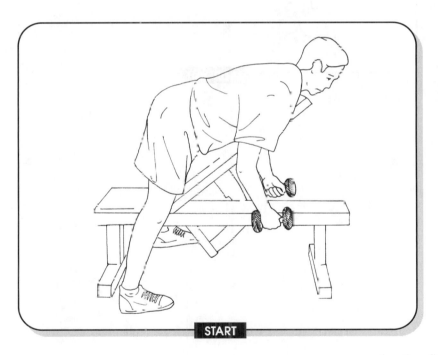

START

(continued)

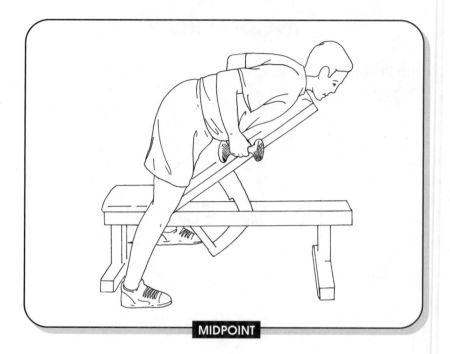

MIDPOINT

INVERTED LEG PRESS

Procedure: 1. Lie face up on an inverted leg press machine and place your feet on the center of the foot plate.

2. Straighten your legs completely and then rotate the safety supports to free the weight.

3. Lower the weight by bending your knees as far as comfortable without lifting your hips off the seat, then straighten your legs completely.

4. When you've completed all the required repetitions, rotate the safety supports back to their original position to secure the weight.

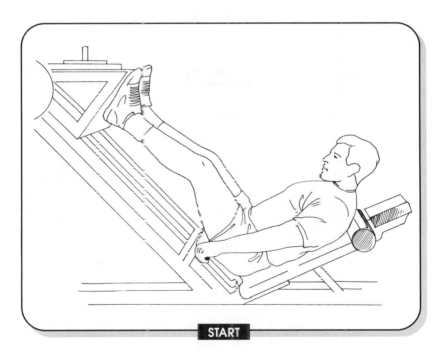

START

(continued)

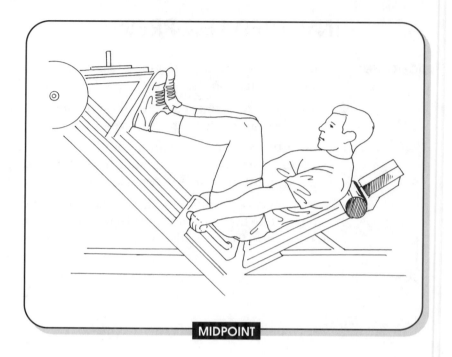

MIDPOINT

LATERAL CHEST FLY

Procedure: 1. Lie face up on an exercise bench and grasp two dumbbells.

2. Straighten your arms and bring them together so that your palms are facing each other

3. Now slightly bend your arms.

4. From this starting position, slowly lower the weights to your sides until your upper arms are parallel to the floor.

5. Return to the start by reversing this motion.

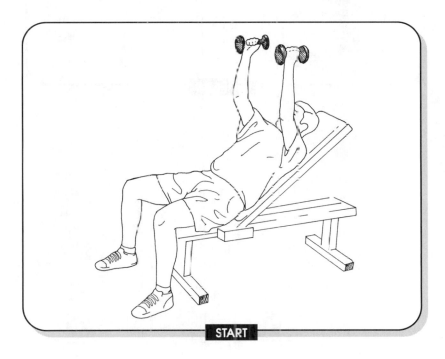

START

(continued)

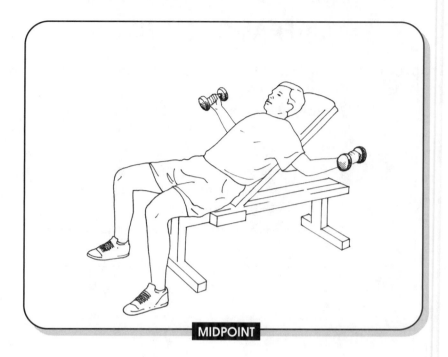

MIDPOINT

LAT PULLDOWN

Procedure:
1. Grasp the bar with a wide grip, palms facing away from you. Your arms should be straight but not locked (start).

2. Pull the bar to the base of your neck by first retracting your shoulders and then following through with your arms (midpoint).

3. Pause momentarily in this position before slowly returning the bar to the starting position.

This exercise can also be performed as a "front" lat pulldown. Pull the bar to the level of your throat in front of your face and then pause and return to the starting position.

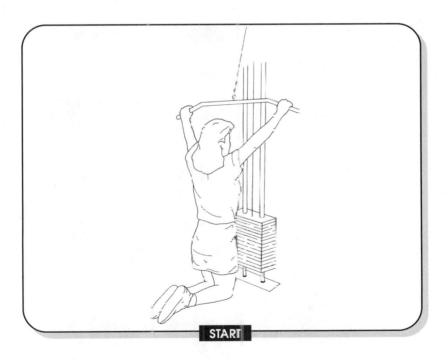

START

(continued)

MIDPOINT

LATERAL RAISE

Procedure:
1. Grasp a dumbbell in each hand and stand with your feet shoulder-width apart. Look straight ahead.

2. With your palms facing each other and arms slightly bent, lift the weights until they are level with the top of your shoulders. Your back should remain motionless throughout this exercise.

3. Slowly return to the starting position.

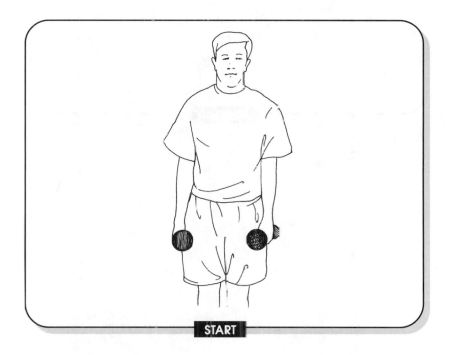

START

(continued)

MIDPOINT

LUNGE

Procedure: 1. With a barbell resting behind your neck, spread your feet about six inches apart.

2. From this starting position, take a big step forward and lower your body to the position shown.

3. Return to the start by shifting your weight backward, straightening your front leg, and taking several small steps back to the start.

4. Perform the next lunge with your other leg as the front leg. Keep your back vertical throughout the exercise.

START   MIDPOINT

OVERHEAD SQUAT

Procedure:

1. Place a barbell behind your shoulders and grasp the weight so that your arms form a 45-degree angle to the bar.

2. Press the weight overhead to extended arms and then spread your feet shoulder-width apart, toes pointed slightly out (start).

3. Take a deep breath and bend your legs in a slow, controlled manner until the tops of your thighs are at least parallel to the floor (midpoint). During the descent, keep your back flat, your chest out, and your eyes focused slightly upward or directly ahead.

4. Drive back to the starting position, exhaling when your legs are nearly straight. During the ascent, look directly ahead or slightly up.

START

MIDPOINT

POWER CLEAN

Procedure: 1.   Squat down and grasp a barbell with an overhand grip, hands facing your body. Spread your feet hip-width apart or slightly wider, whichever is most comfortable. Look straight head and keep your back slightly arched.

2.   Begin the exercise by straightening your legs (not your back) until the bar reaches the middle of your thighs. Continue the movement by completely straightening your knees and back, and then shrug your shoulders; finish the movement by pulling with your arms and then rotating your elbows through so you can catch the bar on your shoulders.

3.   Return the bar to the floor by allowing the weight to drop to midthigh and then slowly lowering it to the floor or rack.

START   MIDPOINT   FINISH

POWER SNATCH

Procedure: 1. Squat down and grasp a barbell with an overhand grip, hands facing your body. Spread your hands apart so that your arms form a 45-degree angle with the bar. Spread your feet hip-width apart or slightly wider, whichever is most comfortable. Look straight head and keep your back slightly arched.

2. Begin the exercise by straightening your legs (not your back) until the bar reaches the top of your thighs. Continue the movement by completely straightening your knees and back, then shrug your shoulders. Finish the movement by pulling with your arms and then rotating your arms around so you catch the weight overhead.

3. Return the bar to the floor by allowing the weight to drop to the top of your midthighs and then slowly lowering it to the floor.

START   MIDPOINT   FINISH

PULLOVER

Procedure: 1. Lie face up on a narrow bench. Your head should be fully supported by the bench—do not let it hang over the edge.

2. To perform this exercise with a barbell, hold the weight with a shoulder-width grip, palms facing away from your body (start).

3. Keeping the weight as close to your head as possible, lower the weight to the midpoint shown and then pull it to the start. Inhale as you lower the weight, hold your breath as your raise it, and then exhale at the finish.

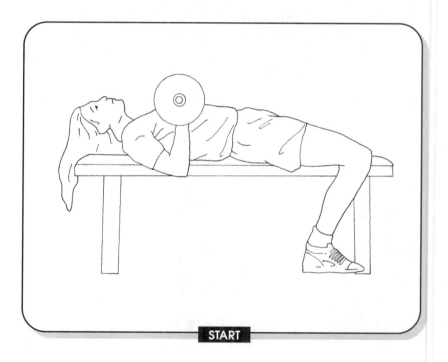

START

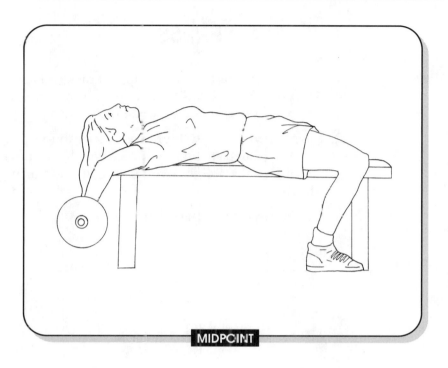

MIDPOINT

PUSH PRESS

Procedure: 1. Remove a barbell from the support racks, placing it on your shoulders as shown. Your elbows should be pointed slightly down and out.

2. Keeping your chest high and your abdominal muscles pulled in, bend your legs slightly (start) and thrust the weight overhead to straight arms (finish).

3. Lower carefully to the starting position.

START   FINISH

ROMANIAN DEAD LIFT

Procedure:
1. Grasp a barbell with your palms facing you and stand erect. (Because you can use heavy weights with this exercise, it's best to begin the exercise by removing the barbell from the support racks.)

2. Keeping your chest out and your shoulders back, bend forward from the waist, letting your knees bend slightly until the barbell reaches your knee-caps.

3. Pause and return to the starting position by reversing the motion.

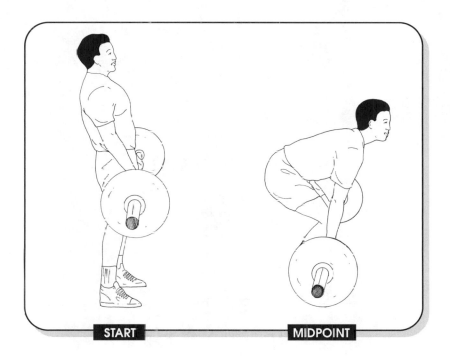

START   MIDPOINT

SEATED CABLE PULL

Procedure: 1. Sit in front of a pulley row machine with your knees slightly bent. Grasp the pulley bar with both hands, thumbs down (start).

2. Begin by pulling your shoulders back, then follow through with your arms (finish).

3. Slowly return to the starting position.

Keep your elbows out to the sides (away from your body) when pulling.

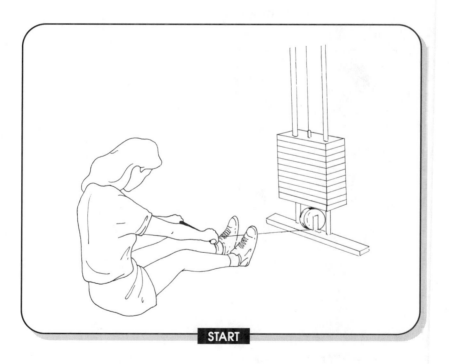

START

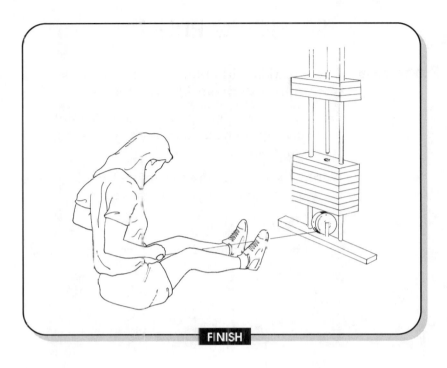

FINISH

SHRUG PULL

Procedure: 1. Grasp a barbell holding your palms facing you and your hands just outside your thighs.

2. Shrug your shoulders as high as possible while extending on your toes and then return to the starting position.

During the exercise, keep the barbell as close to your body as possible and your elbows up and out.

START

MIDPOINT

SIDE BEND

Procedure: 1. Grasp a dumbbell in one hand and stand erect. Place your other hand at your side and rotate both hands so that your palms face each other.

2. Without leaning forward, lower the weight by bending at the waist as far as comfortable; return to the start and bend as far as comfortable in the other direction. Return to the upright position.

3. After you've completed all the repetitions for one side of your body, repeat for the other side.

This exercise may be performed with a weight in each hand, alternating sides.

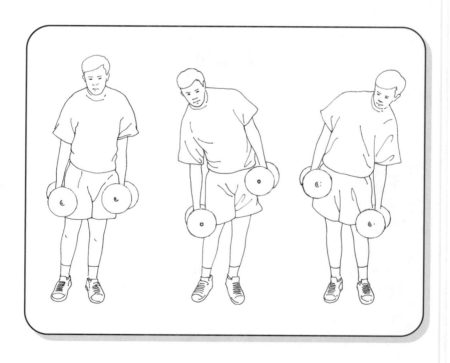

SINGLE-ARM ROW

Procedure:

1. With one arm braced in front of you and one knee resting on a bench, grasp a dumbbell with your free hand and let it hang over one edge (start).

2. Hold your breath and begin the movement by pulling the dumbbell to your upper chest so that your elbow is higher than your chest (midpoint).

3. Pause briefly in this position, then exhale as you slowly lower the weight back to the starting position.

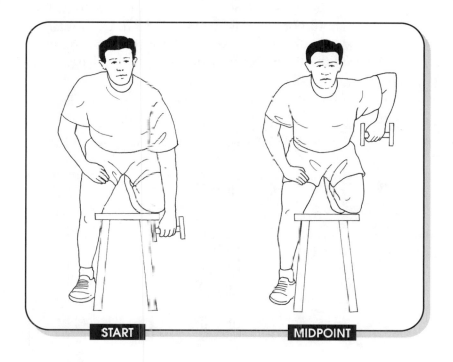

START | MIDPOINT

SPLIT SQUAT

Procedure: 1. With a barbell resting behind your neck, spread your feet about six inches apart.

2. Split your legs apart as far as comfortable, one foot in front of you, one behind.

3. From this starting position, lower your hips straight down until your rear knee almost touches the floor, then return to the start by lifting your hips straight up.

At the bottom of this exercise, your rear knee should not extend in front of the heel of your front foot; it should be several inches behind it. Do not lean forward during the exercise. Perform all the repetitions with one leg before working the other leg.

START

MIDPOINT

STRAIGHT-ARM LAT PULL

Procedure: 1. Stand in front of a pulley row machine with your knees slightly bent. Grasp the pulley bar with both hands, thumbs down (start).

2. Without leaning back, pull the bar down as far as possible without bending your arms. Slowly return to the starting position.

START

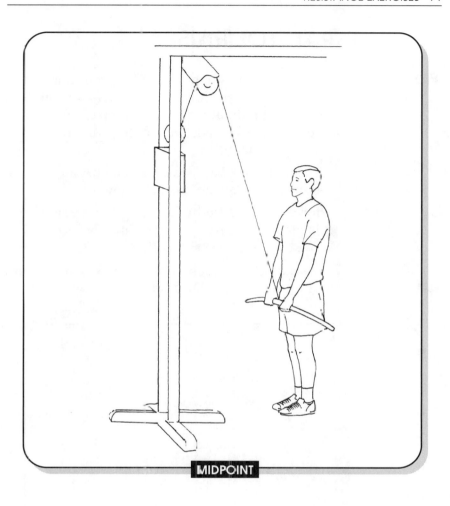

MIDPOINT

TOE RAISE

Procedure: 1. Place your feet on the edge of the machine so that your heels extend lower than the balls of your feet. Place your shoulders under the pads by flexing your legs—the pads should be positioned lower than your shoulders.

2. Keeping your back flat, straighten your legs to assume the starting position shown.

Perform the exercise by lowering and raising your heels through as great a range of motion as possible. Do not bend forward at any time.

For variation, this exercise may be performed with toes in, toes out, and knees bent.

UPRIGHT ROW

Procedure: 1. Grasp a barbell with your hands positioned six to eight inches apart, palms down (start).

2. Pull the weight up to your throat (finish) and then return to the starting position.

During the exercise, keep the barbell as close to your body as possible and your elbows up and out. You can also use dumbbells. If you do, hold the weight with your palms facing you and try to keep the inside edges of the plates touching throughout the movement. Also, avoid the tendency to cheat on this exercise by using the back or leg muscles.

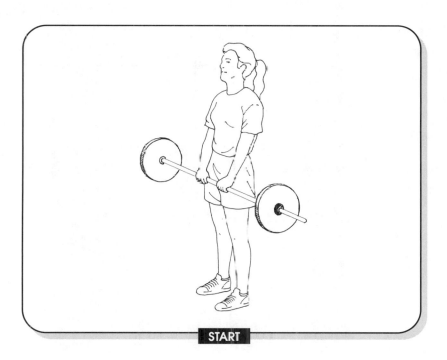

START

(continued)

FINISH

CHAPTER
4

PLYOMETRIC EXERCISES

This chapter shows you how to perform much more than the minimum number of the plyometric exercises you will need to create your own complex training program (see chapter 7). However, be aware that books and even videotapes are limited in how much they can teach you. I advise you to seek the assistance of a qualified instructor when performing any new or especially complex training exercise. Ask the instructor to teach you and a training partner the correct techniques so you can properly assist each other. Also, I cannot emphasize enough the importance of proper footwear. A good cross-training shoe is ideal for almost all plyometric exercises. And always perform plyometric exercises on appropriate jumping surfaces such as a wrestling mat or spring-loaded floors.

Performance guidelines for every plyometric exercise are, of course, beyond the scope of this book. As you become more sophisticated with your complex training routines, you may want to try some plyometric exercises beyond those you'll find in the following pages. Discuss your options with your training coach or seek other sources such as my book, *Jumping Into Plyometrics*, to enhance your progress.

BACKWARD THROW
WITH JUMP TO BOX

Equipment: A box 12 to 42 inches high and a medicine ball

Start: Squat facing the box and holding the medicine ball.

Action: Lower the ball between your legs, then toss it up and back over your head. As you thrust upward to toss the ball, push off the ground and land on the box. Step off the box and collect the ball for the next repetition.

BARRIER JUMP
(HEIGHT VARIES)

Equipment: Four to six hurdles

Start: Begin from a standing position in front of the first hurdle.

Action: Bound over the hurdles, tucking both knees to your chest. Be sure to spend minimal time on the ground between barriers.

BOUNDING

Equipment: None

Start: Jog into the start of the drill to increase forward momentum. As you jog, start the drill with your right foot forward and your left foot back.

Action: This drill is simply an exaggerated running action. Push off with your left foot and bring the leg forward, with the knee bent and the thigh parallel to the ground. At the same time, reach forward with your right arm. As the left leg comes through, the right leg extends back and remains extended for the duration of the push-off. Hold this extended stride for a brief time, then land on your left foot. The right leg then drives through to a forward bent position, the left arm reaches forward, and the left leg extends backward. Make each stride long, and try to cover as much distance as possible.

CHEST PASS

Equipment: A medicine ball

Start: This drill requires a partner. Stand facing each other with your feet shoulder-width apart and your knees slightly bent. Begin by holding the medicine ball with both hands at chest level, elbows pointing out.

Action: Pass the ball to your partner, pushing it off your chest and ending with your arms straight. Your partner catches the ball, returning it to the starting position before passing it back to you.

CHINNIES

Equipment: None

Start: Begin by assuming a sitting position in which your upper body is inclined 45 degrees and your feet are off the ground.

Action: With one leg straight and the other bent so that your knee comes close to your chest, alternate your legs in such a way that they cycle in and out.

CONE HOPS
WITH 180-DEGREE TURN

Equipment: A line of four to six cones spaced two to three feet apart

Start: Stand facing forward, parallel to the line of cones, your feet even with the first one.

Action: Jump and, while in the air, turn 180 degrees so that you land facing the opposite direction. Continue to jump and turn in the air along the entire line of cones.

DEPTH JUMP

Equipment: A box 12 to 42 inches high

Start: Stand on the box with your toes close to the front edge.

Action: Step from the box and drop to land on both feet. Try to anticipate the landing and spring up as quickly as you can. Keep your body from "settling" on the landing, and make the ground contact as short as possible.

DEPTH JUMP
WITH BARRIERS

Equipment: A 12- to 42-inch-high box and a 28- to 36-inch-high barrier, placed about three feet from the box

Start: Stand on the box with your feet shoulder-width apart.

Action: Step off the box and, upon landing, jump over the barrier.

DEPTH JUMP
WITH 180-DEGREE TURN

Equipment: A box 12 to 24 inches high

Start: Stand on the box with your toes close to the edge.

Action: Step off the box and land on both feet. Immediately jump up and do a 180-degree turn in the air, landing again on both feet. For added difficulty, land on a second box after doing the turn.

DROP-AND-CATCH PUSH-UP

Equipment: None

Start: This drill requires a partner. Begin by assuming a
                  kneeling position in which your upper body is in-
                  clined 45 degrees. Have your partner stand behind
                  you and grasp your shoulders to keep you from
                  falling forward.

Action: Your partner should rapidly remove his or her hands
                  so that you begin to drop toward the ground. You
                  "catch" yourself in the push-up position and explo-
                  sively push back to the 45-degree position. Your part-
                  ner catches your shoulders and then repeats the action.

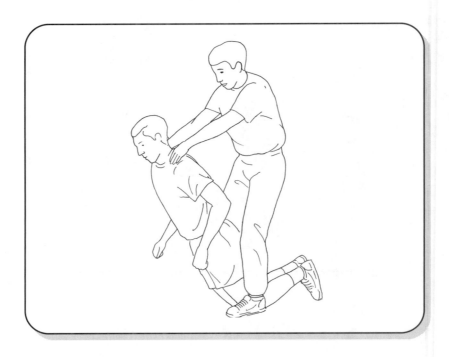

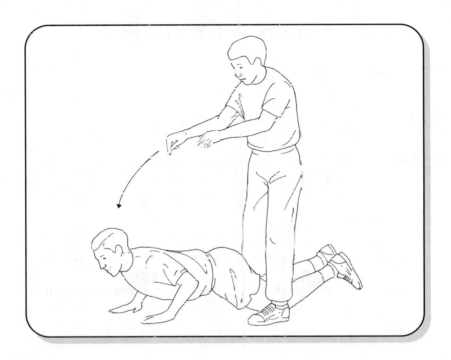

FRONT TUCK JUMP

Equipment: None

Start: Begin in a standing position.

Action: Jump up, grabbing both knees as they come up to your chest, and then return to the starting position. Repeat the action for the prescribed number of repetitions.

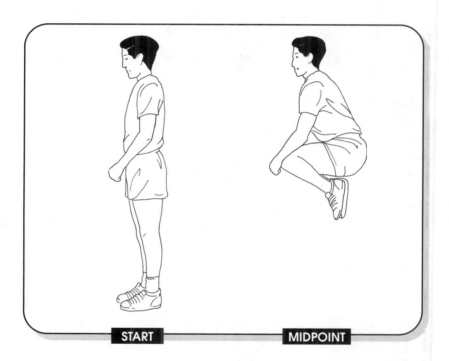

START   MIDPOINT

GLUTE-HAM MACHINE MEDICINE BALL THROW

Equipment: A back hyperextension machine and a medicine ball

Start: This drill requires a partner. Begin by raising your torso into a back hyperextension.

Action: Your partner tosses the ball into your hands, which are extended over your head. You toss the ball back to your partner, partially using the momentum of returning to the starting position.

GLUTE-HAM PULSE

Equipment: A back hyperextension machine

Start: Begin with your hands behind your head and your torso about 10 degrees below your hips.

Action: Extend your back, raising your torso about 10 degrees above your hips in the opposite direction. Return to the starting position by letting the body free fall for just a moment before "catching" the body and raising back up.

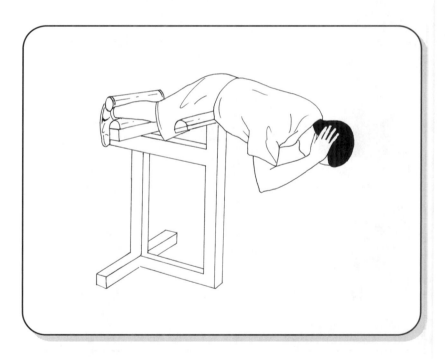

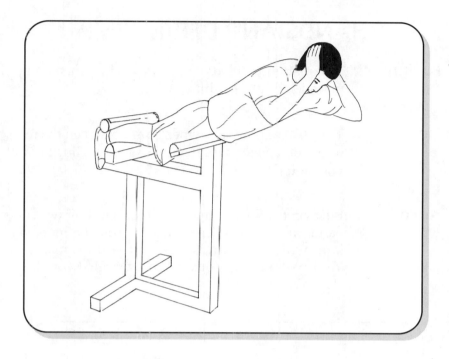

HANDSTAND DEPTH JUMP

Equipment: Two mats or padded boxes, three to four inches high, placed shoulder-width apart

Start: This drill requires a partner. Stand between the mats or padded boxes, with your partner standing behind you, and do a handstand on the floor.

Action: Push off the floor with your hands, landing with one hand on each mat. Then push up off the mats and land with your hands in their starting positions. Your partner spots for you, ensuring that your body stays vertical.

HURDLE HOP

Equipment: Hurdles or barriers (between 12 and 36 inches high) set up in a row, spaced according to ability; barriers should be collapsible in case the athlete makes a mistake

Start: Stand at the end of the line of barriers.

Action: Jump forward over the barriers with your feet together. The movement should come from your hips and knees; keep your body vertical and straight, and do not let your knees move apart or to either side. Use a double-arm swing to maintain balance and gain height.

INCLINE CHEST PASS

Equipment: A medicine ball

Start: Work with a partner and sit facing each other. Lean back at a 45-degree angle, keeping your abdominals tight.

Action: Pass the medicine ball back and forth, keeping the ball in your hands for only a brief time.

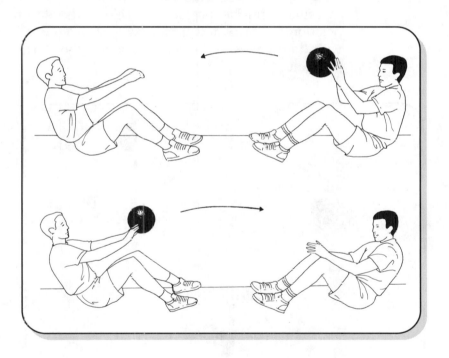

INCLINE PUSH-UP DEPTH JUMP

Equipment: Two mats, three to four inches high, placed shoulder-width apart, and a box high enough to elevate your feet above your shoulders when in a push-up position

Start: Face the floor as if you were going to do a push-up, with your feet on the box and your hands between the mats.

Action: Push off from the ground with your hands and land with one hand on each mat. Either remove one hand at a time from the mats and place it in the starting position or, for added difficulty, push off the mats with both hands and catch yourself in the starting position.

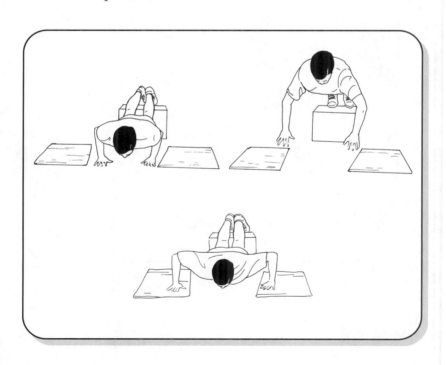

JUMP FROM BOX

Equipment: A box 6 to 18 inches high

Start: Stand on the box with your feet shoulder-width apart.

Action: Squat slightly and step from the box and drop to the floor. Attempt to absorb the landing quickly and "freeze" as soon as you make contact with the floor. Repeat the action for the prescribed number of repetitions.

JUMP TO BOX

Equipment: A box 6 to 12 inches high with a top surface no smaller than 24 inches square

Start: Stand on the ground with your feet shoulder-width apart, facing the box.

Action: Take a short step forward with your preferred foot and quickly bring the back foot in line with your front foot (a step-close technique). Then jump vertically to the top of the box. Repeat the action for the prescribed number of repetitions.

LATERAL BARRIER JUMP

Equipment: A cone or hurdle

Start: Stand alongside the object to be cleared.

Action: Jumping vertically but pushing sideways off the ground, bring your knees up and jump sideways over the barrier. Repeat the action for the prescribed number of repetitions.

MULTIDIRECTIONAL BARRIER HOP

Equipment: Hurdles 6 to 18 inches in height, positioned in the shape of a hexagon

Start: Stand in the center of the hexagon.

Action: Jump out over one hurdle and back to the center. Then continue jumping over the adjacent hurdle, rotating around the hexagon.

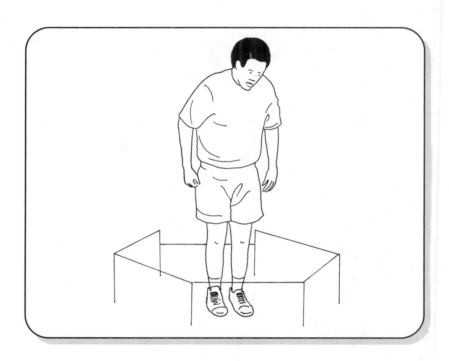

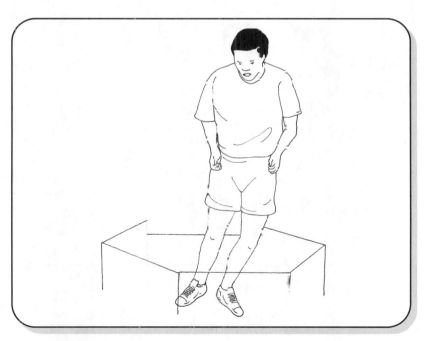

MULTIPLE BOX-TO-BOX SQUAT JUMPS

Equipment: A row of boxes (all the same height, depending on ability)

Start: Assume a deep squat position with your feet shoulder-width apart at the end of the row of boxes. Keep your hands behind your head.

Action: Jump to the first box, landing softly in a squat position. Maintaining the squat position, jump off the other side of the box and immediately onto and off of the following boxes. Keep your hands on your hips or behind your head.

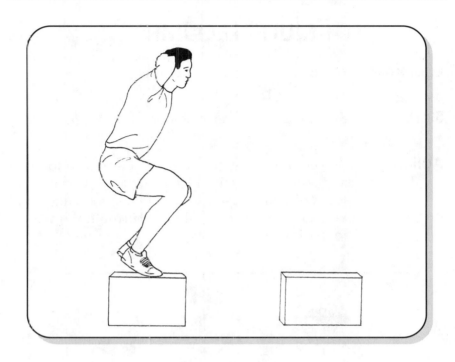

MULTIPLE JUMPS

Equipment: None

Start: Stand with your feet shoulder-width apart.

Action: Lower into a squat position and jump as far forward as possible. Immediately upon touching down, jump forward again. Use quick double-arm swings and keep landings short. Do this drill in multiples of three to five jumps.

NEIDER PRESS

Equipment: A barbell with appropriate weight

Start: Begin with your feet slightly apart and your knees bent. Hold the weight at your chest with your palms facing away. Your elbows should point toward the floor.

Action: Push the bar out away from your chest and up. Your arms should be about 30 degrees above the level of your shoulders. Return to the starting position and repeat for the prescribed repetitions.

OVERHEAD THROW

Equipment: A medicine ball

Start: Work alone or with a partner, and start by standing holding the medicine ball overhead.

Action: Step forward and bring the ball sharply forward with both arms, throwing it to your partner, or if working alone, over a specific distance.

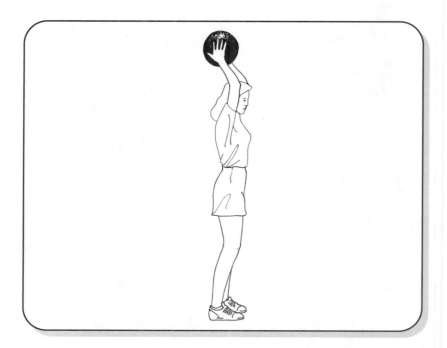

PIKE JUMP

Equipment: None

Start: Stand with your feet shoulder-width apart and your body straight.

Action: Jump up and bring your legs up together in front of your body; flexion should occur only at the hips. Attempt to touch your toes at the peak of the jump. Return to the starting position and repeat.

PLYOMETRIC PUSH-UP

Equipment: None

Start: Begin in the push-up position with your chest on the ground.

Action: Push yourself up off the ground. Both your hands and feet should come completely off the ground. Try to spend minimal time in contact with the ground before executing another push-up.

(continued)

POWER DROP

Equipment: A box 12 to 42 inches high and a medicine ball

Start: This drill requires a partner. Lie supine on the ground with your arms outstretched. Your partner stands on the box holding the medicine ball at arm's length.

Action: Your partner drops the ball, and you catch it and immediately propel it back to your partner. Repeat the action.

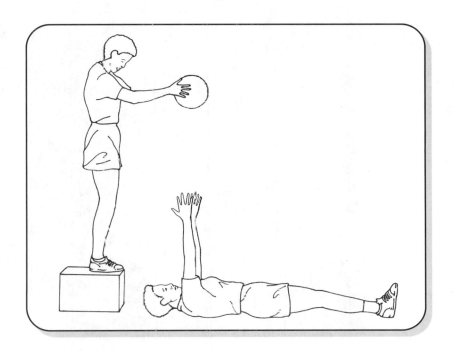

PULLOVER PASS

Equipment: A medicine ball

Start: This drill requires a partner. Lie on your back with your knees bent, holding the ball over your head, while your partner stands at your feet.

Action: Keeping your arms extended, pass the ball to your partner. For increased intensity, your partner can back up to require you to throw farther.

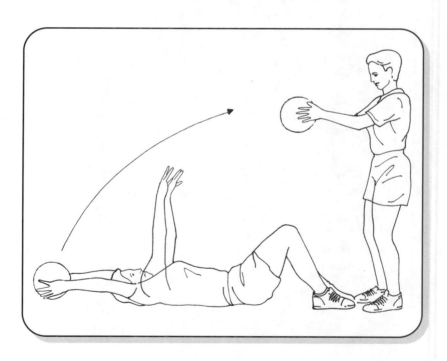

PUSH-UP DEPTH JUMP

Equipment: Two plywood boxes approximately six inches high

Start: The boxes should be placed beside your shoulders. Assume the push-up position with one hand on each box.

Action: Push yourself off the boxes, catching yourself on the floor, then push off again onto the boxes.

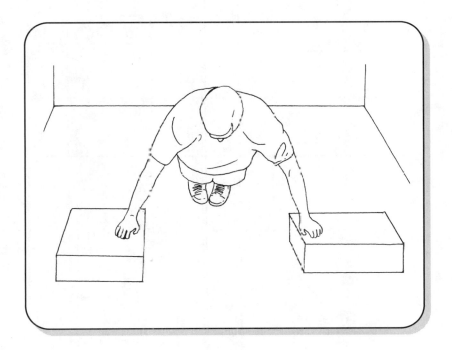

(continued)

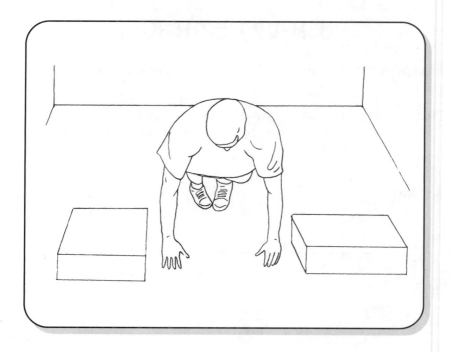

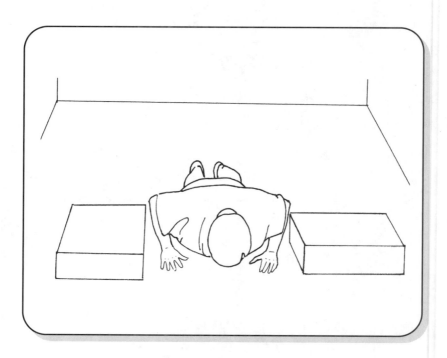

REVERSE HYPERS

Equipment: A treatment table or other table with a level surface

Start: Begin by lying on your stomach with your legs hanging off the end of the table. Grip the sides of the table firmly.

Action: Raise your legs, holding them straight until they are just above parallel to the floor. Lower your legs and repeat the action.

(continued)

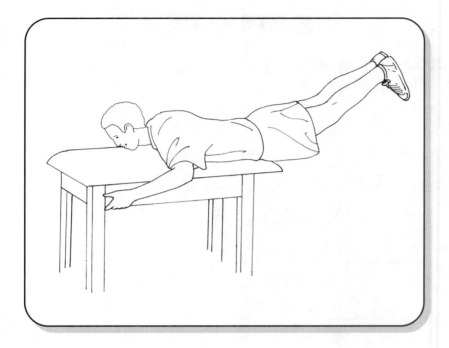

SEATED BACKWARD THROW

Equipment: A medicine ball

Start: This drill requires a partner. Sit holding the ball outstretched over your straight legs while your partner stands behind you, approximately 10 feet away, facing in the same direction.

Action: Raise your upper body, your arms, and the ball as a unit and toss the ball up and back over your head to your partner while keeping your arms extended and your back straight.

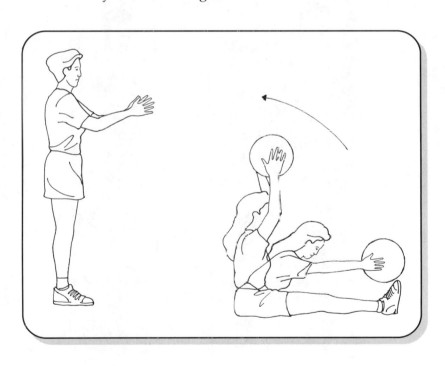

SIDE THROW

Equipment: A medicine ball and a large solid barrier

Start: Holding a medicine ball on your right, stand with your feet shoulder-width apart.

Action: Swing the ball farther to your right and then forcefully reverse directions to your left and release it. You may toss the ball to a partner or throw it against a solid barrier (e.g., a gym wall).

SINGLE-LEG HOPS

Equipment: None

Start: Stand on one leg.

Action: Push off with the leg you are standing on and jump forward, landing on the same leg. Use a forceful swing of the opposite leg to increase the length of the jump and strive for height off each jump. Immediately take off again after landing and continue for about 20 yards. Perform this drill on both legs for symmetrical development. Beginning athletes will use a straighter jump leg; advanced athletes should try to pull the heel toward the buttocks during the jump.

SIT-UP PASS

Equipment: A medicine ball

Start: This drill requires a partner. Sit facing each other two to three feet apart with your knees slightly bent.

Action: Your partner throws you the ball using a chest pass. Upon receiving the pass, lower your torso to the ground with the ball still at chest level. Then sit up and make a chest pass to your partner, who repeats the full sit-up action.

STANDING BACKWARD THROW

Equipment: A medicine ball

Start: This drill requires a partner. Stand approximately 10 feet in front of your partner and face in the same direction.

Action: Hold the ball in front of you, bend forward, and then toss it up and over your head to your partner. Be careful to bend your knees and your hips and keep your back straight throughout the motion.

STANDING LONG JUMP

Equipment: A soft landing surface, such as a mat or sand pit

Start: Stand in a semisquat with your feet shoulder-width apart.

Action: Using a big arm swing and a countermovement (flexing) of the legs, jump forward as far as possible. Repeat the action for the prescribed number of repetitions.

STANDING TRIPLE JUMP

Equipment: A mat or sand pit

Start: Stand with your feet shoulder-width apart, 10 to 20 feet from the mat or sand pit (distance depends on ability).

Action: **Phase One:** Push off on both feet simultaneously and extend through your hips to land on one foot (hop).

Phase Two: Then push from that foot forward to land on the other foot (step).

Phase Three: Then jump from that foot, extending your feet forward as far as possible and landing on both feet on the mat or in the pit.

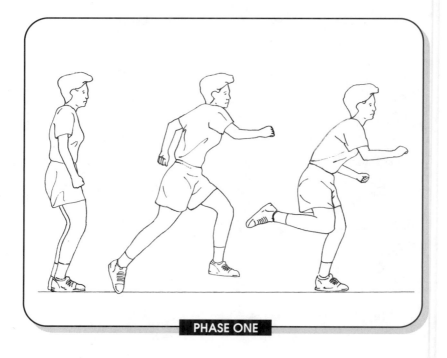

PHASE ONE

PHASE TWO

PHASE THREE

SUPERMAN TOSS

Equipment: A medicine ball

Start: This drill requires a partner. Lie on your stomach facing each other, extending your torso backward so that your arms and legs are suspended and not touching the ground. There should be two feet of space between you with your arms fully extended.

Action: Keeping your arms and legs suspended, pass the medicine ball to your partner from about chin level in front of your head. Continue passing the ball for the prescribed number of repetitions.

THROW DOWN

Equipment: None

Start: This drill requires a partner. Lie on your back on the floor with your legs extended. Your partner stands facing you with one foot on either side of your head so that you can hold onto his or her ankles.

Action: As you raise your legs up to your partner's hands, he or she pushes them down forcefully. You should provide resistance to your partner, catching your legs before they reach the ground and returning them to the raised position. Your partner can push your legs in a variety of directions, ranging from straight forward to more lateral directions.

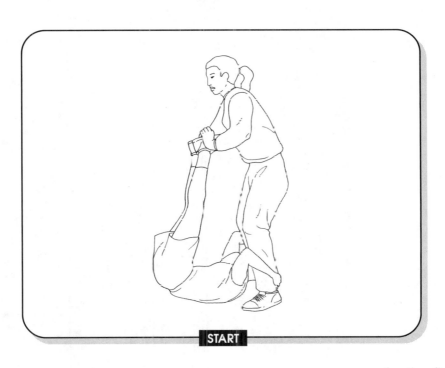

START

(continued)

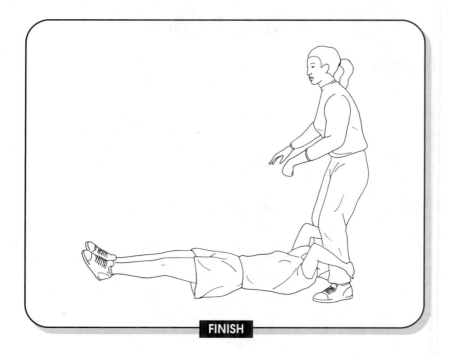

FINISH

TRUNK ROTATOR

Equipment: A medicine ball

Start: Sit on the floor with your legs spread and the ball behind your back.

Action: Rotate to your right, pick up the ball, bring it around to your left side, and place it behind your back again (so the ball makes a circle around your body). Repeat for the prescribed number of repetitions and then reverse directions.

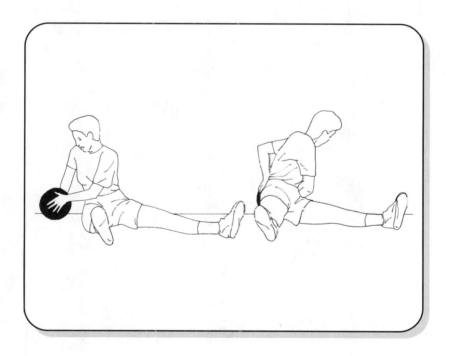

UNDERHAND THROW

Equipment: A medicine ball

Start: This drill requires a partner. Assume a squat position about ten feet from your partner, holding the ball close to the ground.

Action: Keeping your back straight, raise straight up and throw the ball up and out to your partner, using your legs to provide momentum.

VERTICAL JUMP

Equipment: A vertical target provided by a device such as a "Vertec"

Start: Stand with your legs shoulder-width apart.

Action: Use both arms to drop into a ready position for exploding upward. Reach as high as possible.

VERTICAL TOSS

Equipment: A box about 12 to 36 inches high and a medicine ball

Start: This drill requires a partner. Sit in front of the box with your back to it, legs spread apart and straight. The other person stands on the box holding the medicine ball over you.

Action: Your partner drops the medicine ball into your hands. Catch the ball with elbows bent and toss it back over your head to the partner on the box.

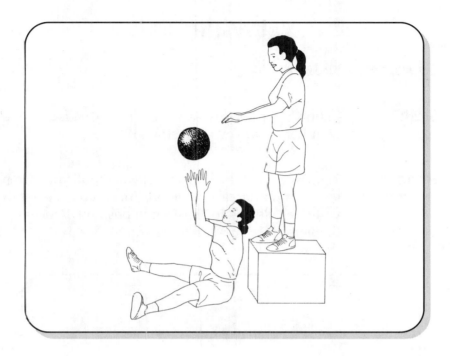

V-UP

Equipment: None

Start: Lie on your back with your arms extended above your head and your legs straight.

Action: Tighten your abdominal muscles and pull your arms and legs up into a V position. Touch your hands to your toes. Return to the starting position. Repeat for the prescribed number of repetitions.

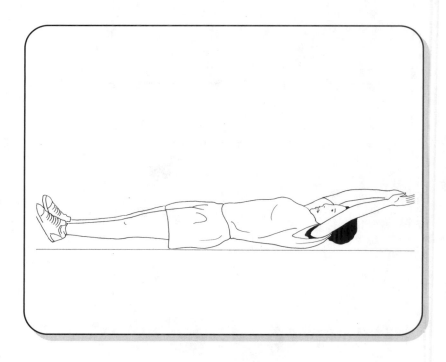

PART III

PROGRAM DESIGN

Athletic development is based on the snowflake principle: No two athletes are identical. Likewise, neither will they begin a training program at the same point or progress at the same rate. Consequently, training programs for all athletes should be as individualized as possible—to the athlete and to the sport. And the importance of individualizing program design grows as the level of competition increases.

The chapters in this part of *Explosive Power and Strength* will familiarize you with the concepts of supercompensation, overtraining and recovery, motivation, periodization, and the complex training coupling system. By knitting these concepts together in a form that fits each individual situation, coaches and athletes can create the complex training workouts that perfectly fit their abilities and ambitions.

CHAPTER

5

INGREDIENTS FOR COMPLEX TRAINING PROGRAMS

Now that you understand the exercise components and physiology of complex training, it's time to begin to show you how to apply it. This chapter will discuss the concept of *supercompensation*, which is the basis of periodization (the subject of chapter 6). It also discusses three other ingredients relevant to success: overtraining, recovery, and motivation.

◆ Supercompensation

Supercompensation is the body's ability to take on stress, recover, and then proceed to a higher level. If athletes are challenged at the end of the recovery phase, they will respond with a level of performance even greater than previously possible. Because this phase of supercompensation can be elusive, the proper amount of rest during the recovery portion is imperative for the athlete to make the greatest gains.

Supercompensation follows the normal course of a training cycle, as shown in figure 5.1. The body starts at some zero point of no stress.

Once it undergoes stress (e.g., a set of an exercise), it drops into a fatigue zone. It hits its lowest point in the fatigue zone, the cessation of the exercise, and it begins to recover. Recovery takes the body back to its zero point, but because the body does not know the exact amount of energy stored for the first exercise, it continues past the zero level and into the area of super- or overcompensation. At this point, the body not only has neural arousal, but also a *physiological overcompensation* of energy stores replacement to aid in the next bout of exercise. This is when the plyometrics portion of the coupling becomes crucial. Because plyometrics emphasizes short bursts of power, it is the consummate complement to the supercompensation phase of the body's reaction to stimulus. This is when the body is most ready to perform these exercises requiring maximal effort for both speed and force.

In the complex training system, an athlete can make the greatest gains within the window of supercompensation. For that short

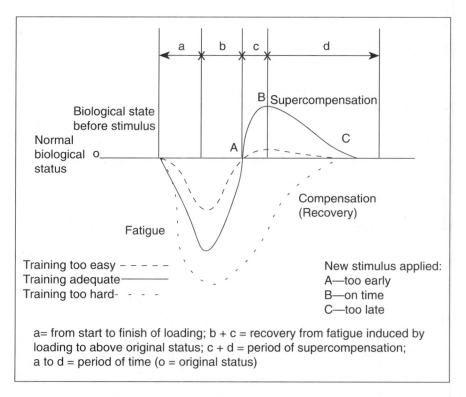

Fig. 5.1. Supercompensation of a training session. Reprinted, by permission, from B. McFarland, 1985, "Supercompensation," *NSCA Journal* 7(3): 44.

period, the athlete can take advantage of a system that is maximally aroused and able to face greater challenges. In contrast, athletes who are brought to this advanced level of stimulation but do not use the opportunity accordingly may find that they have done little or no good and possibly even some harm. If the body is not challenged during supercompensation, beyond making no progress, an athlete may experience a decrease in ability to face a greater stimulus the next time. It's almost as if the body feels that it has been let down and its only source of retaliation is to refuse a second chance at the same disappointment.

The lesson is an obvious one: *The intensities mandated by a complex training program should not be entered into lightly.* Athletes who are ready to make the commitment to working harder will be rewarded with greater progress than they have ever experienced in a conditioning program. Athletes who aren't ready to make such a commitment to all-out hard work should stay away from the complex training regimen and get used to second place.

◆ Overtraining and Recovery

Because the complex training workout is so intense, appropriate rest intervals between pairs of exercises and sets are essential. To get the most out of a workout, the athlete must allow the body to restore the energy supplies within the muscles during the workout.

Determining the appropriate time for rest periods will depend on the level of the athlete. Rest periods of less than one minute will force the muscles into an aerobic state of contraction. Because the muscles will be asked to perform again before they've completely recovered, the loads they will be able to withstand will only be submaximal.

Recovery with the pairs of exercises must be addressed on two fronts: within the pairs and between pairs. Within pairs, athletes need less time to recover because the goal of the second exercise is to capitalize on the excitement generated in the first. The athlete should have enough time to recover so that he or she can continue to train at maximal levels without letting the muscles cool down completely.

The less well trained to intermediate athlete needs significantly less time to recover than the more advanced to elite athlete. Although exact times will vary and should be determined by the coach and player together, table 5.1 illustrates a range of times that should accommodate all levels. It is important to remember that the times are varied because the more advanced athlete will be sustaining loads of much higher intensities, requiring much greater effort.

Table 5.1 Recovery Times		
Level of athlete	**Within a pair**	**Between pairs**
Beginner/Intermediate	0.5 to 1.5 minutes	1 to 3 minutes
Advanced/Elite	1 to 3 minutes	3 to 5 minutes

◆ Motivation

Intensity doesn't always come naturally; it requires motivation. Athletes need two levels of motivation: the initial jump start and the maintenance at a level high enough for adequate performance. The best way to ensure both is to sit down and look at the athlete's value system and set the appropriate goals. What does the athlete want to get out of this competitive season? What level would this individual like to accomplish by the end of high school? College? In the professional or amateur ranks of competition? Would the athlete be happy competing locally? Regionally? Nationally? Internationally?

Once athletes determine where they'd like to be, they need to cross-check these desires with a reasonable level of commitment. How many hours per week are they ready to commit? How much money are they able (or willing) to spend on special equipment, coaches, or time at a camp or training facility? Are they willing to increase their time and financial commitment when advancing to higher levels of competition?

The athlete should also consider his or her support network. Are family, friends, coaches, and teammates behind the athlete's efforts? Do they show an interest (without becoming too demanding) in the athlete's training and results? Do they attend competitions? Do they find ways to support the athlete during the difficult times as well as they do during moments of glory? A lot of athletes are willing to go it alone, with or without a good support system. Sometimes, however, the support network can make the difference between going on or hanging up the cleats for the last time.

Next is the value system. A 14-year-old budding tennis star may not know exactly what her values are for the long run, but she can put some ideas down on paper. What gives this individual satisfaction? Is winning the only reason for playing, or is there an innate thrill in being on the court and feeling the surge of power in a well-hit forehand? Is tennis enough, or is it more important to maintain a balance in life by staying in school, minimizing travel, and planning for college? Would the athlete rather commit to a once-in-a-lifetime opportunity to go for it all and join the professional circuit? These are difficult questions for a young athlete, but on some level, all athletes face tough questions that can only be answered by looking inside themselves.

Many athletes find it helpful to put these thoughts down on paper as they begin to establish goals and objectives. Goals are the outcomes an athlete would like to achieve: a state championship, a college scholarship, a gold medal in the Olympics. Goals can be specific to the short, medium, or long term. *Short-term goals* might include something as basic as "making the team," reaching a qualifying mark for league or conference, or reaching a mark just short of a lifetime best. *Medium-term goals* might center on getting a starting position by your junior year, reaching the conference finals, and then qualifying for nationals. *Long-term goals* might include making all-league, getting a lifetime best in an individual event, or making a national team. Objectives are the paths the athlete takes to accomplish these goals: methods of training, participation in the appropriate competitions and trials, and getting specialized coaching. Often a review of goals and objectives can trigger new vigor in an athlete who is experiencing a momentary low in motivation.

As with the periodization schedule (see chapter 6), goals and objectives should be reevaluated every year to see if the athlete is meeting them. In fact, the athlete should review the established goals more frequently and save the reorganization for an annual review with his or her coach. Reviewing goals and objectives every few months will help keep the athlete on track. It will also give the athlete the opportunity to alter his or her goals and objectives more immediately if training or competitive results necessitate a change.

Sometimes the difference between a true champion and an also-ran is merely motivation. Most athletes train and compete in a comfort zone. They have a certain amount of raw talent, mix it with an adequate supply of conditioning, and produce average results. The athlete who looks beyond mediocrity and is willing to break out of the comfort zone and enter new arenas of training will be the one reaching the higher levels of competition. The pool of competitors will shrink, the need for greater athleticism will increase, and the intensities of the training schedule will have to rise to the occasion.

The more specific a workout is to an athlete's individual needs, the more likely it will keep the athlete motivated. A sprinter doesn't want to do the same workout that his friend is doing to prepare for baseball. Athletes want to know what their body needs to get ahead in their sport. They want to be assessed before training, have a program designed to fit their particular needs, and have their progress charted along the way.

All of these signs point to the same conclusion for the serious competitor: complex training. The complex training program assesses the athlete, individualizes the training, and increases performance. The athlete can participate in the program with very little equipment, respecting her or his financial needs, and complete a workout quickly. In return, the athlete must provide dedication and intensity to the program. If the athlete does so, the results will be dramatic.

CHAPTER

6

PERIODIZATION

Sport isn't a ho-hum affair, and training shouldn't be either. Let's say you designed a static training program that you intended to follow for the course of a year. Two problems arise. First, you'd probably become quickly bored and risk missing workouts. Second, your training wouldn't adequately prepare you for the peak of your season. Smart athletes follow a schedule of training periodization whereby the training schedule is divided into as many as four or more periods. Workouts change with each period so that athletes are prepared to give peak performance just when they need it most.

This chapter explores the concepts behind, and the four phases of, periodization (preparation, precompetition, competition, and transition). For seasonal sports, the periods can be defined easily; they can mirror the calendar year, with the height of the season being the competition phase. For year-round sports (tennis, for example), the season is harder to identify, but the concepts of periodization must be applied to the training schedule nonetheless. Let's examine the four phases of training periodization and how complex training can be periodized.

◆ Preparation

The crux of the preparation period is to prepare the body for the more rigorous training to follow; this period ranges from two to six weeks. High-volume and low-intensity workouts (see table 6.1) are used during this period. Plyometrics and the theories of complex training should be introduced in elementary forms for athletes engaged in explosive, ballistic movements. The full-blown complex training workout will not be explored until precompetition.

Table 6.1 Preparation Phase General Workout	
Exercises[a]	Sets/Reps[b]
Resistance training @ 60-70% of 1RM[b]	2-4/10-15
Plyometrics (Level 1)[c]	2-3/10-12

[a]Exercises should not be paired in this phase. In later phases resistance training and plyometric training exercises will be coupled (see chapter 7).
[b]Suggested numbers only. Program should be suited to athlete's ability and progress. 1RM is the maximum weight one can lift for a single repetition.
[c]See table 7.5 for a listing of Level 1 and Level 2 plyometric exercises.

An assessment should be performed both before and after the preparation period (see chapter 8 for an index of assessment tests). It should also be done for certain facets of the program after each cycle of work. This does not mean every test should be given at every cycle change, but rather testing should be performed to look for *specific* changes. For example, if a volleyball player has a four-week cycle specifically designed for improving the vertical jump to develop spiking ability, she should be tested before and after these four weeks. Conditioning will probably include some basic plyometrics, such as jumps up to a box. The coach can then assess development in this area either by seeing how high a box the athlete can reach or by testing on court in a more applied manner. If the athlete can now spike with accuracy to various areas of the court, this goal has been accomplished. If the athlete is at least spiking cross court and down the line on occasion, some progress has been made.

Extensive technique work is often left for the precompetition phase, but this can be a serious mistake. Athletes have enough to worry about during this intensive period without learning a new technique. Implementing changes, say, in a spiking motion, blocking technique, or any other specific skill should begin slowly and gradually at the end of the preparation period. At the beginning of the cycle, the coach should demonstrate what individual skills the technique requires. Once the athlete has had the opportunity to see the skill and is able to grasp the concept, the coach should break it down into a part-whole training system. The player receives feedback, visualizes performance of the skill, and sets a foundation for perfecting it as he or she enters the next phase.

◆ Precompetition

Once the athlete reaches the precompetition cycle and exercise sessions have grown increasingly more intense, the athlete should concentrate on the execution and tactics of new skills. If the athletes are still dedicated to working on fundamentals upon entering this cycle, they will hit their season of competition before perfecting their technique and will be under undue stress all the while.

In moving from preparation to precompetition, examine the results of the assessment tests. This information will enable the athlete to organize and develop a program aimed at overcoming any physical deficiencies exposed by the testing.

The precompetition phase will be the longest cycle in the player's schedule. It can be several smaller blocks of time, each with its own goal or objective. The goal of one of these periods thus could be focused on developing a special skill or quality, such as the vertical jump, absolute running speed, or lateral change of direction. If increasing running speed is the goal, the athlete now begins to work on the specific components of start strength, acceleration, and transition to absolute speed. If the athlete is the volleyball player still working on the vertical jump, the training will now move to the more intense format of complex training, such as back squats followed by depth jumps.

As table 6.2 shows, this phase begins with building some of the qualities needed for each of these actions: optimal strength, maximal strength, strength endurance, explosive strength, and reactive strength. As the player approaches the end of the cycle and the importance of explosive and reactive strength grows, complex training plays its greatest role. The cycle of work in this area can be 8 to 12 weeks, depending on the level and preparation of the athlete.

Table 6.2 Precompetition Phase General Workout	
Exercises	Sets/Reps[a]
Early phase resistance training @ 70-85% of 1RM[a]	3/6-10
Early phase plyometrics (Level 1)	3/10-15
Late phase resistance training @ 70-85% of 1RM[a]	4/4-6
Late phase plyometrics (Level 2)	4/5-10

[a]Suggested numbers only. Program should be suited to athlete's ability and progress.

◆ Competition

The ability to incorporate complex training into the competition phase will depend on the nature of the sport and the level of the athlete. The better athlete must concentrate on the championships at the end of the season, whereas the beginner first has to make the cut. No matter what the level, the intensities required during the competition season are evident from the workout detailed in table 6.3.

Table 6.3 Competition Phase General Workout	
Exercises	Sets/Reps[a]
Resistance training @ 80-100% of 1RM[a]	3-5/1-3
Plyometrics (Level 2)	3-5/5-6

[a]Suggested numbers only. Program should be suited to athlete's ability and progress.

Track and field is an example of an individual sport suited to using complex training as the season's height approaches. The athlete works toward a series of qualifying championships (e.g., league, area, state, and national). The emphasis during the competition stage is toward peaking during a championship season, which is generally a time window of about four weeks. An advanced track and field athlete seems to work through the meets and competitions that lead up to the championship schedule. Early in the competitive period, he or she is still developing as an athlete and doesn't want to reach peak performance capabilities. The last four weeks of the season will be the time of *athletic realization*, which is the synthesis of all the things the athlete has been working toward in skill development, physical conditioning, and mental training. The four to six weeks prior to this period are meant to be the time for improving as the athlete heads toward a peak.

To accomplish this type of peak, track and field athletes must look at their season as a whole and count backward from the end to determine their conditioning schedule. Once they have counted backward from the championships, they can count forward to plan for them. To anticipate the end appropriately, they should look at their results from last season and forecast where they can expect to be at the end of this one. If their goals are realistic, athletes can adjust their objectives so they complement them with optimal effectiveness. Because track is an individual sport, athletes have the freedom to focus on personal successes and plan their training around them.

Not all individual sports have the same opportunity, however. Tennis is a prime example. The erratic nature of the professional circuit makes scheduling conditioning difficult. With financial and point-system rewards varying haphazardly over the year, as well as the physical parameters of the arena itself, players can't pin down an end to the season.

The best way to organize this type of schedule is to look at all the factors affecting the outcome of the performance. The various surfaces of clay, grass, and hard courts demand a wide range of athletic abilities. Because a player will have to change surfaces over a few weeks, he or she needs to shorten conditioning cycles to match the circuit's demands. Complex training is still possible during the season if, unfortunately, an early-round loss provides a few days off. The athlete just needs to stay aware of which elements of the program are changeable when the competitive schedule makes training possible.

Of the team sports, football may be the most amenable to maintaining a complex training schedule because of the relatively large segments of time between contests. With a week between games, the two to three days needed for strength and power development give the athlete some freedom in scheduling. Depending on the level of competition, football players face a 10- to 16-game season. If the athletes use each week as a minicycle, they can build power throughout the season and still maintain their starting level of conditioning at the end of the season.

At the opposite end of the spectrum is professional basketball. A basketball player's season is more than 80 games and involves continuous travel throughout the country. Essentially, workouts will consist of attempting to maintain strength and muscular endurance. Power development during the competitive season will not be considered because the intensity of the workouts would be too stressful for the athletes to maintain their competitive performance.

◆ Transition

As athletes enter the active rest phase, they return to activities in other sports, leaving the intensities of complex training behind. They may want to do some rope skipping or some other activity for an aerobic base. In the case of track athletes, they can switch events: The 100- to 200-meter runner should try the 400- to 800-meter range. The long or triple jumper should do the high jump or run 200s. The shot-putter or discus thrower should work out with the javelin or do some 60s. In the team sport arena, the volleyball player might play some basketball or even soccer.

The transition phase is also a time for cross-training in the biking, swimming, or water exercise areas. The athlete can do some unweighted sprinting on the treadmill, incorporate some uphill runs, or use a sport kite for resistance. Any activity the individual would not normally participate in during the season, but which is related to maintaining his or her level of fitness, is appropriate.

CHAPTER
7
DESIGNING YOUR PROGRAM

Thus far, we've covered the basics of complex training. You know that the components of a complex training system are resistance training, plyometrics, sprint training, and sport-specific training. You have read about the physiological principles that form the basis of complex training, and you understand that effective training programs use periodization so that the athlete peaks at the appropriate point in the season. The question now is how do you put this all together. That's what this chapter is about.

The following pages show you

- the proper coupling of resistance training and plyometric training exercises that are at the heart of the complex training,
- examples of the individual complex training workouts performed by different athletes at different phases in the periodization cycle, and
- basic workouts for 11 different sports.

The chapter concludes with some blank workout forms for you to copy and use as you design the complex training program that's right for you.

◆ The Process of Designing an Individual Training Program

Complex training programs are highly individualized depending on an athlete's sport, goals, abilities, and health. One of the beauties of the complex training system is that the coupling of exercises that are at the core of each complex training workout can be easily manipulated. This way athletes—by choosing sequences of sport-specific pairs of resistance training and plyometric training exercises—can work on improving specific aspects of their sport while they train their bodies to play the sport.

Naturally, the built-in flexibility of the complex training system makes it nearly impossible to prescribe complex training programs. There is no one-and-only program that works for basketball players, no one-and-only program for gymnasts, and no one-and-only program for tennis players. Coaches and athletes have to design fluid programs that fit their own situations. Luckily, the process for designing a program is fairly straightforward (even if the results of that process yield highly individual programs). The steps necessary for designing a program are these:

• **Step 1: Know what you want from your program, and know how far you are from your goals.** This is where assessment comes into play. Use some of the tests in chapter 8 to find out how you currently stack up, and compare your current fitness and skill levels to where you'd like to be. Armed with this knowledge, you should be able to set reasonable and reachable long- and short-term goals for yourself. Athletes and coaches must also be honest with each other to determine whether an athlete is currently a beginner, intermediate, advanced, or elite performer. This is important because recovery times within and between pairs of resistance and plyometric exercises vary according to an athlete's performance level. Check table 5.1 on page 144 to find recovery times that are right for your situation.

• **Step 2: Determine the periodization schedule for your training.** Do this by counting backward from the date you wish to peak. If you're trying to make the squad, you may need to peak at the tryout camp. If you're a solid performer, you may need to count backward from the date of the championship game. If you play an individual sport, you might pick the premier event in your field as your target for peaking. The peak is at the height of the competition phase. Once you know your peak date, count backward on a calendar to set the dates for your precompetition and preparation phases. The transition phase will, of course, follow the competition phase and precede next season's preparation phase.

• **Step 3: Create complex training workouts for each phase of your program.** Serious athletes know how and when to take care of the sprint training and sport-specific skill training components of a complex training program. If they don't, their coaches certainly do. What is novel about complex training is the specific pairing of resistance training and plyometric training exercises. Tables 7.4, 7.6, and 7.7 provide athletes and coaches with a starting point for pairing sets of exercises for 11 sports. But don't be tied to these suggestions. Creating training programs is more akin to art than it is to an *exact* science. Let the demands of the sport along with the athlete's needs, desires, and abilities—tempered with solid advice from a training professional—allow for individualization in the selection of the pairs of exercises that make up complex training workouts. You'll find table 7.5 a useful tool in this regard. What about the resistance training loads and the number of exercise reps appropriate for each program phase? See tables 6.1 to 6.3 (on pages 148 and 150) for this information.

• **Step 4: Work, work, work!** Attack your complex training regimen and enjoy the results. Throughout the training cycle, take some time to assess your improvement, celebrate attaining your short- and medium-range goals, modify your program as necessary, and enjoy the rewards of your labor.

Let's add some detail to the process.

◆ Individual Complex Training Programs at Work

The following pages contain snippets of complex training programs designed for athletes. They are for different sports, for athletes from a range of ability levels, who are at different periodization phases. These examples will give you insight into the variables that come into play to make each training program unique. They also exemplify the flexibility and specificity inherent in the complex training system.

Table 7.1 is designed for a neophyte female professional tennis player. The young woman is in her early twenties and has no background in training. As this is for her preparation period, she is introduced to plyometrics and resistance training separately. Her body is not yet ready for the rigors of complex training.

Table 7.1 Female Professional Tennis Player (Preparation Phase)	
Exercises	**Sets/Reps/Weight (lbs)**
Squats	3/10/45
Toe raises in four positions	1/12/25
Lunges in three directions (not paired)	1/10/10-lb medicine ball
Lat pulldowns	3/10/55
Biceps pulldowns	3/10/55
Adductor pulls	3/12/20

Plyoball routine:
    Overhead throws
    Trunk rotators
	3/10-15/6-lb medicine ball

Lateral cone hops (three cones)	6/2/body weight
Orthodyne internal/external rotation	3/10-15/4-6
Fastek movement drill	4 times with 30 s rest

Table 7.2 is designed for the precompetition phase of a 16-year-old female high school volleyball player. She is six feet four inches tall and weighs 160 pounds. She has had two years of previous training, but only during the summer months, not in season. She is somewhat familiar with the positions of exercise movements. This athlete has the potential to play Division I volleyball in college if she continues to develop. The program listed below represents a four-week cycle in her precompetition period. She has completed all her preparation work and is ready for the stresses of the program.

A general workout for a Division I college football team is detailed in table 7.3. The pairs of exercises are suited to all members of the team, but the loads have been left out so that each athlete can determine the appropriate weights for his workout.

Table 7.2   Female High School Volleyball Player (Precompetition Phase)

Exercise pair	Sets/Reps/Weight (lbs)
Squats	3/10/55
Jumps to 18-in. box	3/10/body weight
Toe raises in four positions	1/12/65
Net block jumps	3/10/body weight
Romanian dead lift	3/10/45
Back hyperextensions	3/10/body weight
Lunges in three directions (not paired)	1/10/10-lb medicine ball
Inverted leg press	3/12/180
Hurdle hops	3/10/body weight
Lat pulldowns	3/8/65
Overhead medicine ball throws	3/20/10-lb medicine ball
Blocking movement drill (not paired)	3 times

Table 7.3   Division I College Football (Competition Phase)

Exercise pair	Sets/Reps
Squats	3/3
Squat box jumps	2/5
Single-leg squats	2/5 per leg
Single-leg hops	1/15 m
Walking lunges	3/20 m
Explosive step-ups	1/10
Side lunges	3/8
Lateral barrier hops	3/3
Straight-leg dead lift	3/5
Standing backward throws	2/12
Four-way hip machine	2/8
Over and under medicine ball drill	30 s/8-lb ball

◆ The Complex Training Coupling System

As tables 7.2 and 7.3 clearly demonstrate, effective complex training workouts rely on a succession of successful marriages of a resistance training exercise and a plyometric training exercise. Table 7.5 is a menu of various complex training combinations. For each body part trained, the athlete should choose one exercise from the resistance portion and one to match it from the plyometrics portion. (Descriptions of exercises are provided in chapters 3 and 4.) As the athlete builds power over the course of his or her training cycle, he or she should progress accordingly from level 1 to level 2 exercises.

◆ Designing Your Own Complex Training Program

As I've said numerous times, complex training schedules should be created to fit the specific needs of each athlete. But if you're just getting into complex training, you've got to start off with something. To give you an overall perspective of complex training, tables 7.4, 7.6, and 7.7 show you how to design complex training programs for several sports. The tables focus on two major classes of exercises: one for the preparation phase and one for the precompetition and competition phases. Table 7.4 applies to sports that contain a jumping (vertical) component such as volleyball and figure skating. Table 7.6 is for sports that contain a running (horizontal) component such as football and soccer. Table 7.7 is for sports that primarily require upper body pulling strength such as wrestling and swimming.

Table 7.4   Complex Training for Volleyball, Basketball, Figure Skating, Gymnastics

Preparation phase[a]	Precompetition and competition phases
Front squat Front tuck jump	Power snatch or clean Pike jump
Back squat Standing long jump	Split squat Standing triple jump
Alternating dumbbell press Overhead throw	Push press Incline push-up depth jump
Bench press Chest pass	Incline bench press Plyometric push-up
Lat pulldown Underhand throw	Seated cable pull Standing backward throw
Glute-ham raise Seated backward throw	Good morning Glute-ham medicine ball throw
Hip crunch Sit-up pass	Abdominal curl with pulley V-up

[a]Athletes who are just being introduced to resistance and/or plyometric training may not couple resistance and plyometric exercises in the preparation phase.

Table 7.5   The Complex Training Coupling System

RESISTANCE EXERCISES

Shoulders	Chest	Upper back	Lower back
High pull Push press Alt. dumbbell press Upright row Front raise Lateral raise Shrug pull	Bench press Incline bench press Lateral chest fly Pullover	Seated cable pull Bent-over row Single-arm row Lat pulldown Incline row	Romanian dead lift Good morning Glute-ham machine

PLYOMETRICS: LEVEL 1

Shoulders	Chest	Upper back	Lower back

Overhead throw
Underhand throw
Vertical toss
	Chest pass
	Pullover pass
	Incline chest pass
		Underhand throw
		Seated backward
		  throw
		Overhead pass
			Seated backward
			  throw
			Glute-ham pulse
			Reverse hypers

PLYOMETRICS: LEVEL 2

Shoulders	Chest	Upper back	Lower back

Incline push-up
  depth jump
Handstand depth
  jump
Power drop
Neider press
	Drop and catch
	  push-up
	Power drop
	Plyometric push-up
	Push-up depth jump
	Neider press
		Standing backward
		  throw
		Superman toss
		Power drop
			Backward throw
			  with jump to box
			Standing backward
			  throw
			Glute-ham medicine
			  ball throw

RESISTANCE EXERCISES

Lower extremities	Trunk	Total body
Back squat	Abdominal curl	Overhead squat
Front squat	with pulley	Power clean
Split squat	Straight-arm lat pull	Power snatch
Lunge	Hip crunch	
Toe raise	Hip rotator	
Inverted leg press	Side bend	
	Glute-ham machine	

PLYOMETRICS: LEVEL 1

Lower extremities	Trunk	Total body
Standing long jump	Side throw	Cone hop with
Barrier jump	Trunk rotator	180-degree turn
(height varies)	Sit-up pass	Front tuck jump
Lateral barrier jump	Pullover pass	Depth jump
Jump from box	Incline chest pass	
Jump to box		
Vertical jump		

PLYOMETRICS: LEVEL 2

Lower extremities	Trunk	Total body
Standing triple jump	Throw downs	Depth jump with
Depth jump	V-up	180-degree turn
Hurdle hop	Chinnies	Multiple box-to-
Multiple jumps		box squat jump
Multidirectional		Pike jump
barrier hop		Depth jump with
Bounding		barriers
Single-leg hop		

Table 7.6   Complex Training for Football, Rugby, Soccer, Hockey

Preparation phase[a]	Precompetition and competition phases
Hang clean Barrier jump	Power snatch Single-leg hop
Back squat Lateral barrier jump	Split squat Multidirectional barrier hop
Alternating dumbbell press Overhead throw	Push press Incline push-up depth jump
Bench press Power drop	Incline bench press Plyometric push-up
Lat pulldown Underhand throw	Seated cable pull Standing backward throw
Glute-ham raise Seated backward throw	Good morning Glute-ham medicine ball throw
Hip crunch Sit-up pass	Abdominal curl with pulley V-up

[a]Athletes who are just being introduced to resistance and/or plyometric training may not couple resistance and plyometric exercises in the preparation phase.

Table 7.7   Complex Training for Swimming, Judo, Wrestling

Preparation phase[a]	Precompetition and competition phases
Back squat Front tuck jump	Power clean Pike jump
Bench press Chest pass	Incline bench press Plyometric push-up
Lat pulldown Underhand throw	Seated cable pull Standing backward throw
Single-arm row Overhead pass	Lat pulldown Superman toss
Glute-ham raise Seated backward throw	Good morning Glute-ham medicine ball throw
Hip crunch Sit-up pass	Abdominal curl with pulley V-up

[a]Athletes who are just being introduced to resistance and/or plyometric training may not couple resistance and plyometric exercises in the preparation phase.

◆ Tracking Your Progress

After all this reading, I'm sure you're ready to check out the benefits of complex training for yourself. Well, follow the principles described in this book, design your program, and go for it. Use the forms on the following pages to help you track your progress through the different phases of your training cycle.

Preparation Phase Workout			
Phase dates:_____ Long-term goal:_____ Short-term goal:_____			
Exercise pairs[a]	Recovery time within a pair	Sets/Reps/Weight	Recovery time between pairs
------------------			

------------------			

[a]Athletes who are just being introduced to resistance and/or plyometric training may not couple resistance and plyometric exercises in the preparation phase.

Precompetition Phase Workout

Phase dates:_____   Long-term goal:_____

Short-term goal:_____

Exercise pairs	Recovery time within a pair	Sets/Reps/Weight	Recovery time between pairs
------------------			

Competition Phase Workout

Phase dates:_____   Long-term goal:_____

Short-term goal:_____

Exercise pairs	Recovery time within a pair	Sets/Reps/Weight	Recovery time between pairs
- - - - - - - - - - - - - - - - -			
- - - - - - - - - - - - - - - - -			
- - - - - - - - - - - - - - - - -			
- - - - - - - - - - - - - - - - -			
- - - - - - - - - - - - - - - - -			
- - - - - - - - - - - - - - - - -			
- - - - - - - - - - - - - - - - -			

CHAPTER
8

ASSESSMENT

We usually think of assessment as the portion of the training program that occurs after an athlete has been trained. But if you want to know where you're going, you first need to determine where you are. Assessment before and during a training program allows athlete and coach to test various athletic abilities and determine where strengths and weaknesses are.

◆ Choosing Assessment Tests

Depending on the sport, certain weaknesses will be more apparent and may be more important to correct. If this is true, the most helpful assessment tests would be those specific to the sport in question. Jumping ability is crucial to a basketball player. Starting speed is a desirable quality for a serve-and-volley tennis player who wants to get to the net quickly. And the ability to explode through a line is important for a running back.

The best way to assess an athlete is through field tests. The first step is to look at a particular activity to see what skills are inherent to that activity. Once each component has been determined, coach and athlete can match the skills with the appropriate field test. Field test results are then compared with a set of normative data for that test. In the tests that accompany this chapter, the listed norms are from tests performed on elite athletes in various field tests. For purposes of building power, these norms should give the athlete the appropriate ranges with which to match his or her results.

The tests that follow answer basic requirements noted by the National Strength and Conditioning Association (NSCA) as important in test development. Each test is reliable and valid. An athlete taking a particular test three times in one day will have consistent scores, allowing the coach to average the day's scores from the three trials. The tests measure specific elements important to the sport. They are simple and inexpensive to administer to large groups, and they are interesting enough to incite the competitive spirit among athletes. The tests are also relevant in that they contribute to each player's athletic development.

Although general athletic assessment would look at a variety of factors (e.g., flexibility, muscular endurance, aerobic conditioning), the complex training program limits assessment of speed and strength. Speed can be measured in several ways, depending on the type of movement. Sprints measure *linear speed*, which is how fast an athlete can take off and maintain a certain level of speed. Sprint tests are then broken down according to which aspect of speed needs to be measured: the start or the level reached at a certain point thereafter. Lateral direction is examined through tests such as the change-of-direction drill, and various other tests can show an athlete's ability to perform in a multiple-choice discrimination situation, as well as a pure movement test. Power can be assessed by looking at results of different types of jumps. *Vertical power* is determined by results in a standing vertical jump test; *linear power* is tested using the standing long jump and standing triple jump.

Athletes who want to gain an extra edge on the competition have other tests available to them, but these tests violate one of the aforementioned requirements: They're expensive. For example, the amortization phase of the running motion, also known as the period of shock absorption, begins the moment the foot touches the ground and ends when the body's movement downward stops. Assessing the length of the amortization phase would be helpful for the coach and athlete in determining speed, but the test requires a piece of equipment that can cost as much as $70,000—not quite the type of budget most athletes and coaches have available.

◆ When to Test

The tests that accompany this chapter will gauge an athlete's starting point and should be used periodically to continue monitoring the athlete's development. To be most beneficial, assessment tests should be incorporated into the periodization schedule. Athletes should be tested before the season and at the season's midpoint. If the athlete feels up to it, a postseason test is an option once the athlete has had some time for active rest (that is, when he or she is into the transition phase). Testing too soon after peak performance could be overly stressful for the athlete and could preclude an accurate test result and increase the risk of injury during testing.

Injury is an important consideration during assessment. Coaches need to remember that assessment tests can be very taxing for an athlete. If an athlete is recovering from or bordering on a serious injury, not only will the assessment be less useful, it may aggravate the injury. Therefore, assessment tests should never be conducted at the end of a strenuous workout or after competition, and coaches should use discretion in letting an athlete sit out of a particular test that may cause harm.

◆ Using Norms

The following pages detail the equipment needed, procedures, scoring, and norms for eight assessment tests. The norm data chosen represents compilations of figures extrapolated from testing of elite athletes. Because these athletes compete at world-class levels, coaches and athletes must be liberal in their comparisons. If a 16-year-old high school sprinter is falling in the 80th percentile of Olympic competitors, that athlete is probably well on the way to a successful sprinting career. Norms of this caliber can and should be an inspiration to the up-and-coming athlete. They should serve as a goal as each athlete aspires to reach higher plateaus of success, and they should be used appropriately so as not to discourage a younger athlete.

In comparing results to the norms, it's important for the athlete to consider a few facts. First, norms may be grouped according to age, gender, sport, or other variables. Age is chronological, not biological. Thus, two 15-year-old baseball players may be at vastly different stages of development. If they both weigh 140 pounds, with one at a height of five feet eight inches and the other at six feet two inches, it's not fair to compare them. Neither is it fair to compare the athlete who is six feet two inches with a 20-year-old player of the same height. The latter has matured into his height and has had the opportunity to lose the awkwardness common to younger, growing men.

The same is true for comparing athletes of different sports. By virtue of being an advanced athlete in a particular sport, a player will naturally develop physiological strengths and weaknesses common to that sport (or even to a specific position within the sport). A lineman won't win any races against the running back he protects, and the same is probably true when comparing a center to a point guard.

Finally, remember that these tests are based on performances by elite athletes. Where an athlete falls at this time on these tests is in comparison to the very best. Athletes should treat this data as a benchmark for improvement, not as a mandate on success or failure in their respective sports.

STANDING LONG JUMP

Equipment:
- Tape measure
- Chalk

Procedure:
- Draw a starting line on the ground.
- Athlete begins with both feet approximately shoulder-width apart and on the starting line.
- Arms should be used to assist movement.
- Athlete is allowed to use a "countermove" to aid in achieving some elastic strength, and leaps as far as possible in a forward, linear direction.

Scoring:
- Distance traveled should be measured to the nearest half inch at the heel of the back foot.
- Record best of two trials.

Table 8.1 Norms for the Standing Long Jump

% Rank	Females Height (m)	Males Height (m)
91-100	2.94-3.15	3.40-3.75
81-90	2.80-2.94	3.10-3.39
71-80	2.65-2.79	2.95-3.09
61-70	2.50-2.64	2.80-2.95
51-60	2.35-2.49	2.65-2.79
41-50	2.20-2.34	2.50-2.64
31-40	2.05-2.19	2.35-2.49
21-30	1.90-2.04	2.20-2.34
11-20	1.75-1.89	2.05-2.19
1-10	1.60-1.74	1.90-2.04

STANDING TRIPLE JUMP

Equipment:
- Tape measure
- Chalk

Procedure:
- Draw a starting line on the ground.
- Athlete begins with both feet approximately shoulder-width apart and toes on the starting line.
- Athlete should start with a two-footed takeoff with a double-leg push.
- Athlete pushes from both legs, projecting him- or herself linearly.
- Athlete lands on one foot (hop), immediately projects linearly to land on the opposite foot (step), and concludes by jumping from that foot to a two-footed landing (jump).

Scoring:
- Distance traveled should be measured to the nearest half inch at the heel of the back foot.
- Record best of two trials.

Table 8.2   Norms for the Standing Triple Jump

% Rank	Females Height (m)	Males Height (m)
91-100	8.15-8.85	9.80-10.50
81-90	7.40-8.14	9.05-9.79
71-80	6.65-7.39	8.30-9.04
61-70	5.90-6.64	7.50-8.29
51-60	5.15-5.89	6.75-7.49
41-50	4.40-5.14	6.00-6.74
31-40	3.65-4.39	5.25-5.99
21-30	2.90-3.64	4.50-5.24
11-20	2.15-2.89	3.65-4.49
1-10	1.40-2.14	2.90-3.64

VERTICAL JUMP

Equipment:
- Ladder
- Meter stick
- Chalk
- Wall with high ceiling

Procedure:
- Chalk fingertips of athlete's right hand.
- Athlete should stand with right side of body against wall.
- Athlete reaches as high as possible with feet flat and makes a chalk mark on the wall.
- Athlete jumps off both feet as high as possible and makes a second chalk mark.
- Measure the distance between the two chalk marks.

Scoring:
- Distances should be measured to the nearest half inch.
- Record best of two trials.

Reasons for disqualification:
- Any improper procedure in placing the first chalk mark
- Taking a step or shuffle step before jumping

(continued)

Table 8.3 Norms for the Vertical Jump		
% Rank	Females Height (cm)	Males Height (cm)
91-100	76.20-81.30	86.35-91.45
81-90	71.11-76.19	81.30-86.34
71-80	66.05-71.10	76.20-81.29
61-70	60.95-66.04	71.10-76.19
51-60	55.90-60.94	66.05-71.09
41-50	50.80-55.89	60.95-66.04
31-40	45.71-50.79	55.90-60.94
21-30	40.65-45.70	50.80-55.89
11-20	35.55-40.64	45.70-50.79
1-10	30.50-35.54	40.65-45.69

FLYING 30

Equipment:
- Stopwatch
- Marking cones set 30 meters apart to indicate start and finish lines

Procedure:
- Athletes start on their own time, 30-40 meters behind the starting line. Using the lead distance, they should be sprinting at maximal effort as they cross the starting line.
- An assistant gives a hand signal when the sprinter crosses the starting line.
- On this hand signal, the timer starts the stopwatch and stops it as the sprinter crosses the finish line.
- To ensure consistency, the same assistant should be used for all attempts.

Scoring: The average of two trials is recorded as the 30-meter sprint time.

Table 8.4	Norms for the 30-Meter Sprint From Running Start	
% Rank	Females Time (s)	Males Time (s)
91-100	2.90-2.99	2.50-2.59
81-90	3.00-3.09	2.60-2.69
71-80	3.10-3.19	2.70-2.79
61-70	3.20-3.29	2.80-2.89
51-60	3.30-3.39	2.90-2.99
41-50	3.40-3.49	3.00-3.09
31-40	3.50-3.59	3.10-3.19
21-30	3.60-3.69	3.20-3.29
11-20	3.70-3.79	3.30-3.39
1-10	3.80-3.89	3.40-3.49

25-METER SINGLE-LEG HOP

Equipment: • Stopwatch

• Cones to mark start and finish lines set 25 meters apart

Procedure: Athlete starts 10-15 meters behind the starting line. Using a jog run-up, the athlete starts hopping on the dominant leg. The time starts at this point and continues until the athlete passes the finish marker.

Scoring: The best of two trials is recorded.

Table 8.5	Norms for the 25-Meter Hop	
% Rank	Females Time (s)	Males Time (s)
91-100	3.13-3.75	2.70-3.25
81-90	3.76-4.50	3.26-3.90
71-80	4.51-5.70	3.91-5.00
61-70	5.71-6.90	5.01-6.10
51-60	6.91-8.15	6.11-7.20
41-50	8.16-8.90	7.21-7.90
31-40	8.91-9.45	7.91-8.40
21-30	9.46-10.05	8.41-8.95
11-20	10.06-10.34	8.96-9.25
1-10	10.35-10.70	9.26-9.60

FIVE-METER SPRINT FROM A CROUCH

Equipment:
- Stopwatch
- Starting blocks if working with a track athlete
- Cones for marking start and finish of sprint

Procedure: Athlete assumes his or her normal starting or "ready" position. Upon an audible signal from the coach, the athlete moves as quickly as possible past the finish marker.

Scoring: The best two out of three trials are recorded and averaged for the score.

Table 8.6 Norms for the Five-Meter Sprint From a Crouch

% Rank	Females Time (s)	Males Time (s)
91–100	1.32-1.34	1.18-1.20
81–90	1.35-1.37	1.21-1.23
71–80	1.38-1.40	1.24-1.26
61–70	1.41-1.43	1.27-1.29
51–60	1.44-1.46	1.30-1.32
41–50	1.47-1.49	1.33-1.35
31–40	1.50-1.52	1.36-1.38
21–30	1.53-1.55	1.39-1.41
11–20	1.56-1.58	1.42-1.44
1–10	1.59-1.61	1.45-1.47

LATERAL CHANGE OF DIRECTION

Equipment: • Stopwatch

• Three cones set five meters apart on a straight line

Procedure: • Athlete starts at the middle cone. Coach gives signal and points in a specific direction, right or left. Athlete moves to and touches the first cone, then returns past the middle cone (start) to the far cone and touches that one. Then the athlete returns to the middle cone, touching that one.

• Coach starts timing immediately after giving the "go" signal.

Scoring: The best of two trials in each starting direction, right and left, are recorded and the best score in each direction is used for scoring.

Table 8.7	Norms for the Lateral Change of Direction	
% Rank	Females Time (s)	Males Time (s)
91–100	3.22-3.37	2.90-3.05
81–90	3.38-3.53	3.06-3.21
71–80	3.54-3.69	3.22-3.37
61–70	3.70-3.85	3.38-3.53
51–60	3.86-4.01	3.54-3.69
41–50	4.02-4.17	3.70-3.85
31–40	4.18-4.33	3.86-4.01
21–30	4.34-4.49	4.02-4.17
11–20	4.50-4.65	4.18-4.33
1–10	4.66-4.81	4.34-4.49

SQUAT STRENGTH

Equipment:
- Olympic bar with enough weight in plates to exceed maximum effort for one repetition
- Power rack or appropriate squat rack
- Coach and two spotters as assistants

Procedure:
- Spotters take positions on either side of the bar and load the bar with 70 percent of the athlete's estimated one-repetition maximum (1RM).
- Coach assumes position behind the athlete and helps the athlete position him- or herself in the middle of the bar.
- Athlete takes the bar from its resting position with help from spotters and performs a set of 10 repetitions as a warm-up.
- Athlete replaces the bar and waits three minutes before 1RM attempts.
- Coach and spotters load the bar with approximately 90 percent of expected 1RM. Athlete repeats the procedure.
- Increments of 5 to 10 kilograms should be added so that 1RM is achieved within four to five attempts. Otherwise the testing becomes too laborious.

Scoring:
- Athlete must assume a position with thighs parallel to the floor for the attempt to be ruled fair and complete.
- 1RM is achieved when the athlete fails to complete a lift on his or her own.

(continued)

Note: Younger, less well trained athletes should not attempt to score this test until they have established sufficient technique and base strength. Other tables are available for extrapolating 1RM from any number of repetitions up to 10.

Table 8.8	Norms for Squat Strength	
% Rank	Females Weight	Males Weight
91-100	1.41-1.50 × body weight	1.91-2.00 × body weight
81-90	1.31-1.40 × body weight	1.81-1.90 × body weight
71-80	1.21-1.30 × body weight	1.71-1.80 × body weight
61-70	1.11-1.20 × body weight	1.61-1.70 × body weight
51-60	1.01-1.10 × body weight	1.51-1.60 × body weight
41-50	0.91-1.00 × body weight	1.41-1.50 × body weight
31-40	0.81-0.90 × body weight	1.31-1.40 × body weight
21-30	0.71-0.80 × body weight	1.21-1.30 × body weight
11-20	0.61-0.70 × body weight	1.11-1.20 × body weight
1-10	0.51-0.60 × body weight	1.01-1.10 × body weight

BIBLIOGRAPHY

Adams, K., O'Shea, J., O'Shea, K., & Climsten, M. 1992. The effect of six weeks of squat, plyometric and squat-plyometric training on power production. *Journal of Applied Sport Science Research*, 6(1): 36-41.

Allerheiligen, B., Edgerton, V., Hayman, B., et al. 1993. Roundtable: Determining factors of strength—part 1. *National Strength & Conditioning Association Journal*, 15(1): 9-22.

Bauer, T., Thayer, R., & Baras, G. 1990. Comparison of training modalities for power development in the lower extremity. *Journal of Applied Sport Science Research*, 4(4): 115-121.

Behm, D. 1987. Strength and power conditioning for racquet sports. *National Strength & Conditioning Association Journal*, 9(1): 37-41.

Bielik, E., Chu, D., Costello, F., et al. 1986. Roundtable: Practical considerations for utilizing plyometrics, part 2. *National Strength & Conditioning Association Journal*, 8(4): 14-24.

Billeter, R., & Hoppeler, H. 1992. Muscular basis of strength. In *Strength and power in sport*, edited by P. Komi, 39-63. Oxford: Blackwell Scientific.

Charniga, A., Gambetta, V., Kraemer, W., et al. 1993. Roundtable: Periodization—part 1. *National Strength & Conditioning Association Journal*, 15(1): 57-67.

———. 1993. Roundtable: Periodization—part 2. *National Strength & Conditioning Association Journal*, 15(1): 69-76.

———. 1987. Roundtable: Periodization—part 3. *National Strength & Conditioning Association Journal*, 9(1): 16-26.

Christian, V., & Seymour, J. 1985. Specific power adaptations relative to strength-power training. *National Strength & Conditioning Association Journal*, 6(6): 32-34.

Chromiak, J., & Mulvaney, D. 1990. A review: The effects of combined strength and endurance training on strength development. *Journal of Applied Sport Science Research*, 4(2): 55-60.

Chu, D. 1992. *Jumping Into Plyometrics*. Champaign, IL: Leisure Press.

Chu, D., & Vermeil, A. 1983. The rationale for field testing. *National Strength & Conditioning Association Journal*, April-May: 35-36.

Hakkinen, K. 1985. Factors influencing trainability of muscular strength during short-term and prolonged training. *National Strength & Conditioning Association Journal*, 7(2): 32-37.

———. 1989. Neuromuscular and hormonal adaptations during strength and power training. *The Journal of Sports Medicine and Physical Fitness*, 29(1): 9-26.

Harman, E. 1993. Strength and power: A definition of terms. *National Strength & Conditioning Association Journal*, 15(6): 18-20.

Harre, D. 1983. Development of speed. In *Sprints & relays: Contemporary theory, technique and training*, edited by J. Jarver, 71-73. Los Altos, CA: Tafnews Press.

Hedrick, A. 1993. Literature review: High-speed resistance training. *National Strength & Conditioning Association Journal*, 15(6): 22-30.

Kraemer, W. 1985. Sports performance and specificity of training. *National Strength & Conditioning Association Journal*, 7(2): 65-66.

Lundin, P. 1985. A review of plyometric training. *National Strength & Conditioning Association Journal*, 7(3): 69-74.

MacDougall, J., Sale, D., Moroz, J., Elder, G., Sutton, J., & Howald, H. 1979. Mitochondrial volume density in human skeletal muscle following heavy resistance training. *Medicine and Science in Sports*, 11(2): 164-166.

Manning, J., Dooly-Manning, C., & Perrin, D. 1988. Factor analysis of various anaerobic power tests. *The Journal of Sports Medicine and Physical Fitness*, 28(2): 138-144.

Masterson, G., & Brown, S. 1993. Effects of weighted rope jump training on power performance tests in collegians. *Journal of Strength and Conditioning Research*, 7(2): 108-114.

McFarlane, B. 1985. Supercompensation. *National Strength & Conditioning Association Journal*, 7(3): 44-45.

Medvedyev, A. 1989. *A system of multi-year training in weightlifting*, 94-102. Livonia, MI: Sportivny Press.

Moritani, T. 1992. Time course of adaptations during strength and power training. In *Strength and power in sport*, edited by P. Komi, 266-278. Oxford: Blackwell Scientific.

Moritani, T., & deVries, H. 1979. Neural factors versus hypertrophy in the time course of muscle strength gain. *American Journal of Physical Medicine*, 58(3): 115-130.

Noth, J. 1992. Motor units. In *Strength and power in sport*, edited by P. Komi, 21-28. Oxford: Blackwell Scientific.

Rejeski, W., & Kenney, E. 1988. *Fitness motivation: Preventing participant dropout*. Champaign, IL: Life Enhancement.

Salchenko, I. 1978. More attention to speed. *Track and Field Quarterly Review*, 78(4): 34-35.

Sale, D. 1992. Neural adaptation to strength training. In *Strength and power in sport*, edited by P. Komi, 249-265. Oxford: Blackwell Scientific.

Schmidtbleicher, D. 1992. Training for power events. In *Strength and power in sport*, edited by P. Komi, 381-395. Oxford: Blackwell Scientific.

Semenick, D. 1984. Practical applications—testing. *National Strength & Conditioning Association Journal*, October-November: 45-73.

Stone, M., Keith, R., Kearney, J., Fleck, S., Wilson, G., & Triplett, N. 1991. Overtraining: A review of the signs, symptoms and possible causes. *Journal of Applied Sport Science Research*, 5(1): 35-50.

Totten, L. 1988. *The United States Weightlifting Federation coaching manual, Volume II: General physical training for the weightlifter*, 26-34. Colorado Springs: U.S. Weightlifting Federation.

Van Borselen, F., Fry, A., & Kraemer, W. 1992. The role of anaerobic exercise in overtraining. *National Strength & Conditioning Association Journal*, 14(3): 74-79.

EXERCISE INDEX

INDEX

ABOUT THE AUTHOR

As president of the National Strength and Conditioning Association (NSCA) and a frequent contributor to the *National Strength and Conditioning Association Journal*, Dr. Donald Chu is a leading authority on power training and conditioning. Chu has been a conditioning consultant for the Golden State Warriors, Milwaukee Bucks, Detroit Lions, and Chicago White Sox as well as a consultant for the U.S. Tennis Association and the U.S. National and Olympic Synchronized Swimming Teams. He is owner, director, and consultant to individual athletes at the Ather Sports Injury Clinic in northern California.

Dr. Chu, who earned a PhD in physical therapy and kinesiology from Stanford University, is a professor emeritus of kinesiology and physical education at California State University, Hayward.

He is a registered physical therapist, a certified athletic trainer through the National Athletic Training Association, and a National Strength and Conditioning Association–certified strength specialist. He has received many honors, including the NATA's Most Distinguished Athletic Trainer Award in 1995, and the NSCA's President's Award for Service in 1993. In 1978, his only year as a head coach, Dr. Chu was named the Far Western Conference Track and Field Coach of the Year.

Improve vertical and linear jumping ability

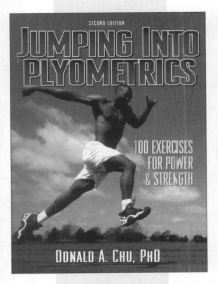

Book

Boost your athletic ability to new heights with the 100 plyometric exercises in *Jumping Into Plyometrics*. These proven exercises will improve strength, power, speed, quickness, and jumping ability while also helping you develop better coordination and balance.

Renowned power training and conditioning expert Donald Chu presents the latest research on plyometric training and provides the most complete collection of plyometric exercises and drills. Chu's instructions and examples will help you build the ideal plyometric program for your sport and your specific training needs.

1998 • Paperback • 184 pp
Item PCHU0846 • ISBN 0-88011-846-6
$15.95 ($23.95 Canadian)

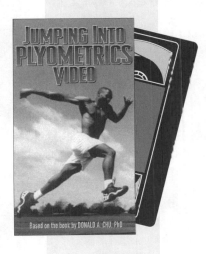

Video

Shows athletes at any skill level how to perform 21 plyometric exercises and how these exercises can be applied to training regiments for a variety of sports.

1993 • VHS • 35 minutes
Item MCHU0246 • ISBN 0-87322-509-0
$29.95 ($44.95 Canadian)

HUMAN KINETICS
The Premier Publisher for Sports & Fitness
www.humankinetics.com

Prices subject to change.